Karma In the flesh!

Chapter 1

Growing up we was always was told you had to work hard for what you wanted, and make sure your family was always good. Even though our family was pretty small the love that we had for each other was unconditional; I would do anything for them and I want to make them all proud being we was from the hood and for some reason I felt I just couldn't let them down. My mother she was in and out of jail steady trying to get her life on track. She had her demons as we all do, so disrespect was never and option. Don't get me wrong she did work at first and then the money got good an my father told her she didn't have to work he want her at home with his children (I remember him telling the story) , but hell we was from a viscous ass city St. Louis ahh chew you up and spit ya right out, so she did the best she could with us. Thank God for my AT (auntie) she was the one who kept us all together. She was so busy taking care of me and all my other siblings along with my mother I don't think she even wanted kids, its like she never could catch a break when it came to my mom. I don't know what we would of did without her she was truly a blessing and I can never repay her for the things that she did.

My Father Big E was the man to everyone in the streets, but me for so many reasons. He did make sure we always had food on the table no matter what an the bills where paid we live comfortably I really must say but shit wasn't always right and I would be the one to get us out the game for good. Numbers where my specialty so I always figured finding the best deals was gonna be my main objective. My Brothers never really told me what they were doing so I knew they would be surprised as hell when I came to them with my proposal, but being who they daddy was I just knew they asses where following in his footsteps and they couldn't turn down my offer. I was book smart thanks to my AT and street smart thanks to my Mom and Big E.

Big E had the shit all set up for my brother of course like my mom doing time for his ass wasn't enough. I don't see how he didn't fought himself for all the bull shit he put my mom's in I mean don't get me wrong I know we our own person and we make our own decisions but damn my pops did her dirty and I found it starting to get hard to forgive him for it. Being I was his only girl and ain't give a damn about us being twins being he came out seconds before it made me the baby(I knew it was due to being the only girl of course), Big E would do whatever to make me smile. I just felt like he was trying to buy my love due to the resentment he knew I had for him. I don't give a damn how much money he made or none of that materialistic ass shit I needed my mother and father just like every girl did hell my brothers did too. He really wanted them to be kingpins for whatever fucking reason, your suppose to want your children to be better than you, not like you. It was then I made up my mind that if I had kids following in the family footsteps would not be an option. It's crazy my dream was going to law school and becoming a successful lawyer and maybe even a judge, a girl really had big dreams and due. Of course, my family would support me becoming a lawyer after all I would become a better accent to a family addicted to the street life. I just always wanted more for everyone not just myself. That was my problem I always had to give a fuck.

"Honey, are you sure you want to do this? I mean you always wanted to go to college , you'll be one of few in this family to actually go to college. Not to mention how far you will get in life!" My A-T asked and stated, as if I didn't think this over a billion times.

"Yes A-T I'm positive I think me doing this a be a good choice for not just me but the family and if things work out as planned I will be able to go after my dreams without Big E help."

"Baby that's what this all over you don't want your "FATHERS" help, you are so damn stubborn child I tell you, Niecey he wants nothing but the best for you all why do you act that way with him, he loves you and your brothers"

This lady was always trying to take up for his ass! " No A-T it's not the only reason but it is in my top 5 since you want to put it that way! Stop taking up for him all the time y'all praise the ground his black ass walk on!

"You know what I'm done questioning you, you right it's your life this a decision to make. I know you love your family but honey don't put your dreams off no one you understand me you said you have a plan so you make sure you stick with it and stay focus got dammit, you are truly your mommas daughter!"

That had to slipped out I know because she never even spoke on my mother referring to me! I didn't know if I should have took that as a good or bad thing so I just excused myself and shook out, whole time thinking; I just didn't get it he turned your only sister out and you think he's a damn GOD, yeah he was named after one but he was far from the only love he had was for money and the only thing he had a passion for was the fast life.I wanted everybody out for good. My plan was solid and I was very confident.

"Man N I really can't believe your not going to college after all the shit you talked about leaving the hood and getting away exploring the world, what happened man! This has to be good so I'm ears, now bitch spill it now!" Nasirah said why literally shaking me to death!

"DAMN, RAH-RAH chill, yo ass know you included in on this damn plan as well, know I can't deal with people like you can, you're a natural." I said why rolling my eyes and pushing her off, of me laughing so hard." Crazy thing about it Rah-Rah don't even know the half of the roll she will be playing, I know that our brothers where to busy with making moves as always so they would have to step in when needed but only finance wise. they didn't want us talking to anyone about anything so they made it our business to become best friends, and I would say we were like sisters being we both where baby girls we clicked right off.

It was strange man we were both living comfortably an still we could not stand the street life(me way more than her I can say), it was so demanding and made me paranoid. Like seriously, always worried, and constantly watching my head it was just instilled I guess you can say. I wanted to live safe and comfortable. I knew I would need assistance so of course my sis Rah-Rah would support whatever I wanted to do, she was so loving and full of life.

"Ok I want to start a business! I know school would have been great but it just seem so selfish for leaving everybody an I'm the only one gaining from the situation I want us all to grow as a family, I want us all to have more!" I waited for Rah-Rah response but she just looked at me with one of her deep looks eyebrows all arched in the air like what the hell you getting at so I continued.

"I know we have everything, but don't you get tired of worrying about if we a get call about somebody getting caught or that even worse having to go identify the body of someone we loved." "Me going to college is going to take years to get anything from it when all we have to do is take a couple courses or some seminars and be way well off!"

Rah-Rah finally said, "ok I think I follow where you going but continue I see you put a lot more thought in to this being you taking us all in consideration, but your life is for you to live not to make us happy, I told you stop worrying about everybody an focus on self, then you come back and help when your able, but I'm listening continue please!" She said why rolling her eyes from disbelief.

"Man here you go preaching and shit, I just need you to be the face of it all honestly you so good with people man I don't see how you do it being we be caged an isolated from soci.....

"Awwww shit! Baby say less, we going to celebrate an I don't care about none of that bull shit you bout to say, drinks on me and I want you to dress up for me(she said as if she was my man) you spend way too much time worrying about everybody else and not enough time worrying about you! Now if you want me to work for you, I have a few conditions, and this is one of them!" Rah-Rah said without taking a breath and completely cutting me off.

"Damn can I get it out first, and I ain't going to no damn club with yo ass why you keep....

"Oh yes the fuck you is going! We need to celebrate my new job as your spokesman!" Rah-Rah said with a real serious intense look letting me know she was about business.

"Ughhhh you killing me right now Rah damn you not even letting me say nothing, damn"

"And I told yo good hearted ass to say less!, you want to put off college and seeing the world, just to stay in this viscous ass city we call home, what more is it you trying to say, I know your plan solid, but go ahead please continue, I'm not making a good impression on my first day"

Thinking to my myself I fucking loved my friend; she knew what I was thinking and how I was feeling with me not even having to say anything. She truly did understand me, hell she was the only person that understands me! "Ok baby you win, I'll dress it up for you should I even ask where we are going or is it a surprise?"

"It's a surprise and I really think you are going to enjoy it well you should really try to enjoy it and don't be all up tight either."

"Bitch don't do me I ain't up tight, you out of all people a really say that shit to me."

"I'm just excited for you man you always see the good in everything an trying to help, I just want you to have a good time."

"Fine you knew I was going to go anyway you irk so damn bad."

"You sure man, I can help you with some paperwork or something I can be an assistant as well I ain't gotta just be the face as you say I can put in work for my spot!"

"Rah-Rah shut da fuck before I change my mind, this not just about me this about us and baby your work is cut out for you already trust me, yo ass was never just getting off that easy! Good thing you took the offer before I finish telling you everything." I said why laughing

"Bet bitch I'm done with it then, we party today an all work tomorrow, now don't forget something nice, right an tight for me!"

CHAPTER 2

"Man bitch the club is fucking lit!" how the hell you manage to get us in here? I kept asking myself

" I told you, you was going to enjoy it who don't like Future" Rah-Rah yelled over the music why we was dancing in circles.

Of course VIP was the place to be two fine as young girls and not to mention the should out form Mr. Future himself. We were really enjoying ourselves and I don't think everybody really enjoyed that.

Rah-Rah must have read my mind being she finally got her ass off the damn people furniture. "hey I think it might be time for us to head on out the vibe starting to change, and I ain't even been drinking."

"you sure Rah man you seem like you was having so much fun and I think the energy shift was me you know I don't like being in the spot light and they kind of put our ass on blast!"

"Naw it most def aint you, you just confirmed its time to go is all that is. Come on let's see if we can spot Nas and E before they spot us heading to the door." Rah Rah said reassured me.

We stood up glancing the crowd and of course Rah Rah nosey ass found them first.
" Lets see they riggggght over der you see em all in the cut trying to blend in and shit, they kill me man everybody know they asses in here no matter how bad they don't want them to, you want to just shoot them a text saying we ready or you want to do a lil walk through rich homie style,' { I be feeling like the man when I walk through}' before we shake."

" Fuck it wo knows the next time we a get to go back out let alone another night like this one. We might as well see who all really in here and it aint like they asses aint watching us like personal security." Referring to both of our over protecting brothers. I couldn't believe the answer I was giving Rah Rah but I knew she really wanted to be seen before we left she loved the attention.

" I cant believe you down for the walk trough now we can see who really was up in here before we leave. Lets see if we can find some joints before we get snatched up." Rah Rah said why laughing, but knowing she was serious as hell.

We was walking hand in hand in a line formation not to lose each other in all the craziness. You can say we barely made it halfway around damn club before some lame ass dude grab a handful of my crouch and tried to literally pull me to him. Before I knew I was punching his as in the neck followed with a stiff ass left hook, I dropped his ass right where he was standing gasping for air. " don't you ever put your fucking hands on me you fucking clown!"

Rah Rah now standing behind me tapped me on the shoulder as she pointed our brothers coming our way like bulls seeing red, she grabbed me and continued making our way to the door. Damn how the hell I lose my cool so quick I gotta start thinking man, I don't even know who the hell that nigga was. Rah Rah made sure she reminded me of my thoughts we didn't make it out the door before she started.

" You really have to chill man, I can't believe you just did that nigga like that, we don't who that is, what if they see us out one day and want to retaliate." Rah busted out laughing before she could even finish. " Do I even need to ask how he grab you that made you react that way, I seen you in act but damn bitch I think you been holding out on some lessons or training I don't know about."

Rah really knew how to break the damn ice, I couldn't stand holding my laugh in any longer. " its not funny bitch so let me stop laughing. He literally tried to snatch me up by my pussy bitch, never have I ever had a mf try me like that in my life. I just snapped out man."

Before I could finish my sentence thing one and thing two came busting out the door frustrated as ever from looking for us.

"Before yall start cussing us out lets walk and talk please, im getting paranoid" Rah Rah said before either of the angry birds could get a word out.

"Well why the fuck would yall ass just fly the fuck up outta der like that knowing we was fucking looking for yall ass, Rah you looked me dead in my fucking face and fucking pointed at me, what the fuck just happened in der." Nas asked sweating out of breath with a vain popping out the side of his head.

"Fuck all that why the fuck yall silly asses just ain't fucking text us man. We agreed to the shit for what if yall was just going to do what the fuck yall wanted to do anyway, that's the unnecessary ass drama I was talking about, niggas out here trusty man!" Ethan said looking at us all intense.

"Did yall even know them niggas man what the hell happened in der man, that's what took so long we was waiting to see they next move and dude was pretty embarrassed and upset." Nas asked trying to get in site on what just took place.

"Hell fucking naw, that bitch ass pussy grabbed a hand full of my coochie so he got a mouth full of my fucking fist and I made sure he chocked on it. I was defending myself how he gonna get mad at that!" I asked damn near in tears cuz I knew what they was getting at.

"You kicked his ass bitch fuck all that you held your own, now I bet you be the last female he ever try to snatch up in the club. Don't start that crying and shit. You straight just beat a grown man ass and you crying, I love you so much." Rah Rah said trying to hold her laugh in acting all sarcastic like she was about to cry.

We where almost at the car when all hell broke loose, Bow Bow Bow, schhhhhh, ahhhhh, tires smoking people yelling and the bullets just kept ringing like they were never going to stop. This is how a night at a STL club would usually end, if not a fight then a shot out. Sad to say but my black people can't seem to go nowhere wit out being violence.

All the yelling and the craziness brought me back to reality, it literally felt like an outer body experience, everything and everybody moving in slow motion and watching everybody even what it seems like to be myself ducking and running for cover. I stood in total disbelief as I watch the scene play out in front in me. I knew the night would end crazy at the club but never would I think it would end like this I mean we never even came outside let alone to the club. Our brothers always wanted to keep us from the clubs and parties and now I can honestly see why.

"Fuck!!! No no no no no, yall gotta help me get her to the car please don't let her die on me not here not like this!"

I had to snap back once I realized he was talking to me and I was looking at my best friend laying there damn near dead. I grab the keys and ran to spot where the car was parked, it seem like I made it to back to them wit in a blink of an eye, we were so close to the damn car. They handled her so gently yet with swift. Ethan jumped in the driver set and stashed the guns under the seat, as I jumped in the passage side. Twin instant was really something. Watching Rah Rah laying in back set I knew I had to do something, "Help me get her shirt off we have to try and stop the bleeding she losing to much blood."

Damn man get your shit together Nas thought to himself, look at her she so focused and yet here I was acting fucking helpless. How the fuck am I post to wrap my mind around the fact my baby sis, my heart, my world was fighting for her fucking life and I couldn't even get my head out my ass.

"Snap out of it and help me get her shirt off!" I said as I took mines off as well to help stop the bleeding. "Use as much force as you can with out hurting her just to slow the bleeding down, we don't want to do too much because we don't know if it was a clean shot in and out" I noticed they both looked at me surprised, I don't know why they know A-T told me everything she knew about the nursing people back to health, considering who our damn family was. I check for a pulse and I could barely find it. Just as I was going to pull my hand back in disbelief, we pulled right up to the emergency room doors. The car was barely stopped before I jumped out and ran into the ER grabbing the first stretcher and person in scrubs I seen " you have to help save my sister please she is dying please!"

We sat in that emergency room for what felt like a lifetime I called my A-T for the much-needed support. She was the only one who could make you see the bright side in any situation. the clock was becoming one of my worst enemies. I couldn't stop myself from pacing back and forth watch the damn thing. What the hell is taking so damn long, just as the thought crossed my mind the lucky handpicked nursed, I grabbed came out looking somewhat relieved. So I knew she had to have some kind of good news.

Hey honey my name is Nurse Karen we never really got the proper introduction. I just wanted to give you and update as soon as possible we were able to stabilize her and slow the bleeding down, we did have to revive her once so the we need her first of kin to sign so papers in case we have to again. The shot was not a good one, but she is definitely a fighter. We still need to do surgery as well to remove the bullet, which is another reason why we need her family here for consent.

I had to stop her right then he lips were moving but I don't think I was understanding everything correctly. I gave her a firm look and asked her very stearyl, "You do know how long we been sitting in this waiting room right?" everything about my body language said defensive and aggravated.

"Yes ma'am you never left her."

"Exactly we been the only ones who been here with her and you mean to tell me you don't think we her family."

"No Honey it's nothing like that, I am not saying that all I was just simple asking what your relation to the patient was again, she said shoot A-T a look for help.

Of course A-T stepped in just in time. They are my niece's ma'am I am the next to kin if you are needing family consent, no need to get baby girl all worked up they are first cousin and very close they even call each other sisters. And I am pretty sure she is still worked up over everything that happen. I truly do apologize Nurse Karan and thank you for the update, please keep me informed and I will be right here when you are ready for me to sign those documents.

I looked at her with amassment because she was truly an Angle. She knew Nas and Rah Rah didn't have anyone and she put everything on the line for them. If the hospital found out, we were lying man it would be jail time

Oh! well if that' s the case I will be right back with those documents for you to sign.

" Honey I know this all is ruff for you but you have to try and …. Keep calm, they are doing all that they can trust me, don't you lose your faith you hear me you pray like you never prayed before you pray like its your own life you praying for and let God do his work." A-T said so gently yet so stern, she was firm believer in God and his plans for us in life.

" I know A-T im sorry I know you risking a lot for us doing this, she just really caught me off guard, like if her family wasn't here it was going to go a different way, we been here all this time and she come back with that kind of update what the hell they doing back der!"

" oooohhhh I see where you at, we got God on our side honey and those kind of people I usta tell you about are long gone out of hospitals trust me she is going to be fine, you want to go walk and talk why they get the papers ready" A-T asked with concern

" No lets wait you, they already think she aint got nobody and we been sitting here all night!"

The lady must have been reading A-T's mind after she came flying around the corner with the papers showing her where to sign she recommended that we go get some fresh air been I haven't been outside since I drugged her out to help get Rah out the car.

"No I am fine, I want to be right here when you come back with the next update." The lady nodded her head and walked off back to the OR.

"Nas bra hit the blunt! Them niggas gonna pay for this shit trust me, I don't give a fuck if I have to conduct my own mfn investigation trust me they ass gonna feel your pain bra if not worst!" Ethan said looking at his friend in a state of mind he never seen him in before.

" Man Lil E,...how the fuck I let them niggas get up on us like, i should have been paying more attention, I knew they fucking coming after them how could I be so fucking stupid bra!" Nas asked hitting the blunt like it was his last. He was really beating his self up over everything that just happened.

" Nas you have to stop bra we was both slipping, we was to busy trying to chew they fucking heads off instead of just checking to make sure everything was ok. We got her here and we got them niggas the fuck up off of us they could ok kill all our asses out der! " Ethan said taking the blunt an making sure his friend knew he did all that he could in the situation

" Yeah you right Bra good thing we did double tip the bouncers, and I was just so fucking mad man she knew we was on they asses and she shook us she don't even go to clubs how the hell she miniver through a damn crowd like that." Nas couldn't get the look on her face out his head it was priceless, she looked like a kid that got caught off the porch after the street lights came on and your mommy on the porch with a belt bout to beat yo ass.

"Here man get the blunt and what the hell you smiling at you starting to creep me out." Ethan asked breaking Nas thoughts.

" Her face... bra when she seen us, we made eye and she knew she was in trouble but it was so funny low key." Nas told him why hitting the blunt and passing it back.

" Yeah she really is something man, and they asses together is truly a force to be recked with." Ethan said giving a lil laughing thinking about the look on Rah face when she seen them coming trough the crowed looking for them.

"Come on Bra lets head back in and see if they got some kind of update." Nas said.

" Hey yall what's the word, you get a update yet" Nas asked me and A-T

"Man hell naw not really nothing you a want to hear trust me, her ass aint do shit but piss'd me the fuck. Coming out here being all cute and shit!" I couldn't wait for they asses to get back I missed them low key.

"Yall really have to excuse her she is a little upset, I don't know what the hell then gotten into this child. She really isn't herself right now, im sure you all can understand." A-t said jumping in to save them from me ranting. "They just wanted to make sure we all were family and they had me sign some papers saying that I was the legal guarding and emergency contact. They also said only 3 of us are allowed up here why she is still on black out, I haven't finished the list yet but they due to me being the guarding i have to be one of the 3."

Ethan instantly stepped in, "I'll go don't even think about it, I got some business to tend to anyway, and Nas aint in his right state of mind right not he needs to be here with Rah if anybody do!"

"Man what you mean you got business to handle and I aint in my right state of mind nigga yo business is my mfn business." Nas said very defensive.

" It aint nothing like that man I just going to put my ear to the streets to see what the word is" Ethan explained " I know you Bra and its ok to show emotion at a time like this be here for your lil sister man she all you got."

" iight bra make sure you call me if you hear anything, be safe out der bra I love you and thank you for everything." Nas said while giving they handshake followed by a one arm hung.

"Can yall please walk Lil E to his car so this damn child can get so air, she don't want to leave because she think she going to miss something, she needs so air she is in here flipping out on these poor people." A-t said before they could say they good byes Inside.

" Come on big head lets walk ya brother to his car, you A-t goona make sure Rah is good" Nas insisted on getting her out the ER.

" Fine but I hope yo ass parked close Lil E cuz I aint walking no dan country mile I know it wasn't no damn parking spots!" I said trying to break the ice and put everybody at ease.

" Damn Lil sis so its like that, just bring ya water jug head ass, and make sure you can keep up." Lil E said in a joking way as we all headed out the door.

" Man Y'all I ain't even going to fake it them niggas feel me this so foul ass shit. Not only did them niggas know yall was females they seen yall with us and just thought we was some kind of random ass niggas, huh yeah they bitch ass most definitely got that shit off." Lil E was most definitely on some bullshit and at this moment it was nothing we could do that a stop him he looked at Rah like a sister so I can only image the force to be reckoned with.

"Mannnn lil I'm on yo ass you get on any mfn thing with out me and you know I cant get to you if something pop off, if anything bra we need to play this shit smart and do like you said handle our own investigation. Pressure bust pipes so that all we applying trust me give me some time Bra, I just need to get my head right I'm literally ready to kill anybody I think had something to do with this shit but we can't do that." Nas said knowing his best friend like the back of his hand.

"Where the fuck did yo ass park at, this that bullshit I was talking about yo water jug head ass be known what you doing." I said trying to change the subject but remind them I was still walking with them and I didn't want to hear they deam hitman talk.

" Aw shit look like you spoke it up, would you look at that" Nas said catching the obvious hint I was giving, I hated knowing niggas business just me the necessary shit to keep me safe.

"Bet you got my word Nas Bra I most definitely see where you at." Lil E told Nas, they did they lil hand shake hug and then turned to me and gave me a hug then looked me dead in my face and said "iight big head them niggas gonna feel our pain baby and I can promise you that, I know you hurting." Kissed me on the forehead and jumped in the car.

I knew he felt I was hurting it was something about being twins I guess, its always something that happened between us since we were little. I could never hide the way I was feeling from my brother, not to mention him being the evil twin. I didn't know if it was a good or bad thing us getting revenge. It really made me feel some type of way but know they would pay in blood and who was in the way was in for it, they clearly wanted us dead so why should I care if them and theirs go, then you gotta look at it in a logical way, we beefing with fucking ghost and they cant just ride around fuck the city up over some bullshit I caused that's to much blood on my hands and I cant have that on my conscious.

"Man Nas I am so sorry I really did mean for any of this to happen you do know that right, I feel so bad it's all my fault"

"Hey stop and look at me, I don't want to ever hear you say that bs again do you hear me, don't blame yourself for this shit them mfn niggas is cowards you hear me 3 rules no kids, women, and elderly. Them niggas knew what they was getting they self into when they pulled that shit. You was defending yourself who the hell he think he is Donald Trump walking around grabbing all on you like that, I'm glad you got to his ass before I did."

I not going to lie I never ever looked at Nas in a sexual way and I honestly didn't understand why I was starting to now. I mean don't get me wrong he was definitely some eye candy and everything you could think you would need in a man, she he took care of Rah and they mother before she passed from cancer. What the hell is wrong with me he trying to make me feel better and the only thing I can do is think about jumping this mans bones.

"Did you hear anything I just said, you just completely zoned all the way out on me?" Nas asked being me back.

"Yeah I got you stop blaming myself I understand where you at."

"Good now lets see if we missed anything in the short time we been gone." Nas stated.

"Man we must really be incessant tonight." Nurse Karen state, as we all walked into the Er together.

Nas nudged me and gave me an I told you so look

A-T stood up and asked straight forward " what news do you have for us, it hasn't even been that long did surgery go ok,is she stable?"

A-T approach started to scare me, she was right we hadn't even been going 30 mins and she was already back from the OR something had to be wrong.

Karen took a breath before she spoke " you all may want to take a sit."

A-T was on a roll tonight "no thank you Karen we will stand can you just tell me what's going on with my niece please" she beat me to the punch.

Karen nodded her head and began speaking "We where able to locate and remove the bullet, she lost a lot of blood and she went into shock."

I could feel my soul leaving my body and the room stated to spend, Karen ass was right I should have took a damn seat. Nas caught me mind fall and sat me in the seats next to us. I was out.

" I told you they were like sisters right, I think that's a better out come than I was expecting honestly. Now Karen you mean to tell me she slipped into a comma, how what happened that fast." A-t asked sounding confused.

"She lost a lot of blood ma'am, we really did try everything I promise you we did." Karen said sounding so sincere.

"I don't think you should be making any promises at a time like this Ma'am no disrespect but that's my lil sister and I don't want you out here telling us no bs. What do you all plan on doing to make her come out of this comma" Nas jumped in sternly?

" Thank you nephew, you took the words right out of my mouth" A-t chimed in.

"All we can do is wait for he to come around honestly, she will come too when she is ready. You all just come and sit and talk with her, the more you all make her brain respond to things the better." Nurse Karen said sadly, " Now we will be moving her to a different floor you all will still be her only visitors until further notice, and only two of the three of you all will be able to spend the night. When we get her room number we will let you all know when we are ready to transport her and you are more than welcome to follow." Karen turned and walked away heading back into the OR.

Man it felt like I had been hit by a truck when I finally came to we where out of the ER and what looked like a room. I quickly came back too when I seen my own friend laying in the hospital bed.

"Damn Nas how long have I been out?"

"not that long honestly you needing the rest." Nas said looking out the window of the hospital window.

" I did all that hooping and hollering and I still don't know what is going on, I thought she was telling us she was dead man, Thank God she still with us."

" She in a comma, and they don't know how long it a be before she come out. We gotta keep coming and visiting her so she can come back to us."

" What you mean come to visit, I can stay with her Nas, I know you still have business to handle out side of all of this, your head is about a million and one places and you know she is in good hands with me. You can trust me with her I promise I won't leave her."

" How about we just do shifts I planned on spending the nights with her anyways she the one I usually tell about my day, she always knew what to say."

" ok that sounds like a plan to me that way someone is always with her, she won't get the chance to slip away from us."

" A-t when home yo grab you some clothes I guess she already knew you wouldn't be leaving anytime soon. Im going to head out to meet up with your brother before he dose anything stupid, I know his ass ain't been sitting still for this long. He found something out by now and this hospital aint giving me a signal. You want me to wait for A-t with you are you think you cool."

I just wanted to understand how his brain was processing so much at one time an yet he looked so calm and relaxed, its was so sexy yet scary he did show any sign of emotion.

" I told you not to worry right? Now go and handle business, Im not leaving her noting is that important at this moment."

"keep that big head up and stop beating yourself up its not your fault, ill see you when I make it back." Nas said and gave me a innocent forehead kiss.

Chapter 3

"Man we need to find them bitches and them niggas and finish that job off, them niggas had to packing in the club they ass didn't even make to the car to get down on us like that!" Jstacks said looking at his face in the mirror for the thousand time.

" Man bra claim yo ass down we don't even know them hoes from a can of paint that's what got us in this bullshit in the first place, yo ass tripping." Mellow told his brother

" Fuck them bitches the street talk and we gonna find they asses before them niggas try and retaliate" Jstacks said thinking out load so his brother could hear.

" oh believe me you know I'm riding with you right or wrong I just wanted you to know that shit last night wasn't cool, you broke the rules bra its basically us against everybody." Mellow said to his brother making a very valid point.

" I know bra you know how I get when I get that liquor and that X in my system, we still gotta get them before they get us, nobody is safe." JStacks was all about his respect that was one thing he demanded.

" say less you know if don't nobody got you, I got you!" Mellow and Stacks dabbed it up and went they ways.

* *

" what you got for me Lil E, tell me something good baby I know you ain't going to let me down!" Nas said as he embraced Lil E followed with they handshake.

" Man bra the niggs post to be a fucking connect on the damn east side, the Bar Tender got me hit said he had been tricking his money all night and talking shit."

" Ok I didn't think you find all that shit out, you wasn't playing about that investigation I see." Nas said proudly

" man honestly she hit me up to check on me, said she hear all the commotion and shit that went on and was making sure I was good, she invited me over and we was just chopping it up, she didn't even know we was the niggas in the shot out bra." Lil E inform Nas with a little more detail.

" Damn so she kept you still all this time, I like her ass already bra, but how she know where the niggas from do she know them are something I don't get it." Nas was still confused on how she knew so much about the niggas if she was just a Bar tender, how the hell she know the niggas was a connect. " how she know the niggas was the connect bra?"

" Bra the nigga tried to holla at her and when she ain't go for him he started blowing her down, apparently one of Bouncers know of him on the other side put her on game tell her she was tripping she should of holla at him."

" You think you can figure out that bounce name at that way we can see where them niggas like to hang out at." Nas was ready to go to war with the city and he wasn't stopping until her got the right person.

"Man Bra you don't think that might look kind of suspect I told you bitches just be talking she ain't know she was talking to the mf getting shot at. But the nigga was a big something if I hear it again I will remember. And you know that nigga Sk a get us hip on that end he said he called you to make sure we was good too." Lil E said reminding Nas of they homeboy the bouncer.

" Yeah you right and she might be referring to the nigga he was at he door with he was hella big and I don't usually see em over here that's why we bout had to tip a lil more." Nas said getting his head together. " you know I don't get no service in that hospital man I know I missed all kinds of damn calls."

" its cool Bra they ass followed up with me, I handled it trust me!" Lil E said assuring Nas he made the right decision by staying with his sister.

" iight cool let me call SK ass and see what it is he wanted. I hope this nigga got some information for us and not just checking on us like your fine ass Bartender was" Nas said trying to lighten the move.

"aw I see you got jokes huh, well her fine ass did give us a start so I can't even be mad at her for that" Lil E said giving Nas a playful nudge.

****

"Damn Bobby you mean to tell me you don't even know the niggas are you serious right now. How the hell they get a pistol in the club if you aint know them, you mean to tell me you let these niggas get past you in with some mfn heats." Mellow asked real intense.

"Man I'm telling yall niggas I picked up a shift for my peoples, i don't even like working on that side of the water cuz of shit like that always bound to happen. I can't believe you niggas was really shooting at some Ghost and on top of that you want to pull that shit on the other fucking side, yall niggas aint even from over der." Big Boddy said with animosity shooting Jstacks and Mellow a look that could kill.

JStacks knew it was bigger than Big Boddy and he could do nothing but respect him for sticking to the code of the streets, but the code was also killed or be killed and JStacks had a feeling Big Boddy knew something or he told something, either way it wasn't sitting right with him so Big Boddy had to go.

" Damn Big B its like that now, you gonna switch up on us for some lame ass Hoe! We post to be better than that." Mellow shouted.

Boddy seen things were going left quickly and he said , "Naw niggas it ain't like that, I just don't know shit about the bitches, I told you that was my first night working at the club I ca hit my dude up and see if he remember anything or try to see if he heard something, his ass always working."

"Bet and you know I got you on the money tip it aint no pressure." JStacks said giving Bobby a friendly pound.

When they finally made it back to their car the Jstacks and Mellow both looked at each other and said at the same thime " That nigga know more than what he saying."

"Man Bra that shit just gave me the mfn chills, that's how you know this shit is real, he said we beefing with fucking ghost like he know who the mfn niggas is. Im a kill this nigga if he play us and I promise you that." Mellow said getting more aggravated by the minute.

" I don't believe he know the niggas Mell, but I do think the fat as fucker know more that what he saying, Bobby about his money at the end of the day it may cost a pretty penny but he can come in handy...."

"If his fat ass don't cross us first I told you bra you think them niggas give a fuck about us its me and you vs everybody he a take our mutherfuckin' money and still play our silly asses. How he even know we was the niggas shooting aint none of that shit just sit right with me, we gonna have to watch his fat sneaky ass im telling you bra." Mellow had to make his brother understand the decisions his brother made came with consequences and this just may have been one of them.

Big Bobby made sure to pull right off when he made it to his car he didn't want to give them anytime to follow him and most importantly so he could call his boy SK and see what information he could get on the big tippers from last night.

Ring Ring Ring....

"Yooooo.... Talk to me Big B and don't tell me you fucking quit after your first night on the other side." SK saying in a joking manner knowing he was going to hear from Big Bobby sooner are later.

" Man these niggas tryna finish that job they started with yo peoples...

"Wow wow wow wait a min Big B I got you on the car phone im dropping my lil peoples off let me get right back with you so I can bump into and we can rap about it face to face you know how I do business lil bra." Sk never knew why niggas just start bumping they gums as soon as a mf pick up that's some federal as shit.

"light Big Bra get at me, you know the streets already been talking." Big Bobby was hoping to be reminded him, if the Boyd brothers where paying he knew them Tippers a be paying way more outta respect for the situation. He didn't want to leave the Boyd's waiting to long either and case any suspicion them niggas was reckless and he aint want no kind of beef with they asses.

* *

"Damn yall speak of the Muther fucking Devil himself! I gotta take it let me put it on the car phone he got something watch, just hold tight." Sk told Lil E and Nas ."Yooooo.... Talk to me Big B and don't tell me you fucking quit after one night on the other side."

" Man these niggas tryna finish that job they started with yo peoples...

"Wow wow wow wait a min Big B I got you on the car phone im dropping my lil peoples off let me get right back with you so I can bump into and we can rap about it face to face you know how I do business lil bra."

"light Big Bra get at me, you know the streets already been talking." Big Bobby said before hang up.

"Now why the fuck niggas always want to just start talking I cant stress that shit enough....

Everybody said it at the same time... "THAT'S SOME FEDEARL ASS SHIT" and laughed right after.

They let SK continue, " see that's why yall my mutherfucking niggas if them niggas!"

"aye big dog gone head and holla at yo peoples he seem like he was in a rush, you better get him hip quick if you plan on keeping him on the team, but let him know we got him on the money tip, dude eyes has lit up after we tipped his ass let him know its plenty more of where that came from." Nas said to SK dabbing it up

" on me big dog that call sounded a lil to urgent if you ask me you called it down, make sure you get at me when you hear something you know we got you too!" Lil E said dabbing after Nas and jumping out the Danali truck.

Sk let the window and said real seriously " yall know yall don't owe me shit we peoples what I look like! Faces up ill hit yall in a min!" and he pulled off raising the window up giving a head nod.

Ring ring ring....

"whats the word where you want me to meet you at?" Big Bobby asked SK

"we can meet at the club we need to talk about your future employment with the company anyways, I know last night was a lot with it being your first day." Sk told Big Bobby trying to see where his head was at, niggas was always thinking for the moment and never the long run, he though to himself.

"im in route now, and one night aint gonna scare me off I made more off tips then I did in along time, you know im all bout my paper big bra that's why I called..

"iight I a see you in a few lil bra I aint tryna cut you off I got a call coming in" sk said and hung up

Big Bobby was looking at the phone confused shock his head and head to the club.

Damn that nigga know he can talk I see I gotta get lil bra all the way together if I plan on keeping his ass around Sk said out loud to hisself.

* *

" Damn Big bra you sill aint heard from that nigga Big B yet, it been damn near a week, how long you think it take to find out some information the hoes we was fucking with gave us more information than his ass did." Mellow said to his brother Stacks

"Yeah you right its been more than enough time I was just tryna make sure I wasn't the one tripping. Let me call his ass right now." Jstacks said to his baby brother.

Ring...

"Yo Stacks what it do Og, I was literally just calling you, I know its been a min but I got something for you I don't think its much doe, I know I said they was Gosht but damn.' Big B said trying to sound as convincing as possible.

" its cool Big B I been doing my own foot work as well I been meaning to get back at you about that paper too, but what you got for me." Stacks said

" well only thing I got really is the niggas or the plugs on the WestSide, they got money, and most importantly they respected. A bitch told me they was looking for me not even knowing it was me she was talking about!" Bobby said real excited

" what you mean Big B, what the bitch say." Stacks asked sounding confused.

"Man the niggas put word out who ever knew anything about the niggas that shot at them and they peoples they was paying. She said she knew I worked at the club but aint nva seen me and just wanted a cut if I knew something for telling me. Bitches is sneaky Bra im tryna tell ya." Big Bobby said to Stacks hoping he remembered the Bar tender he tried to talk to at the club that night.

Stacks didn't trust Big Bobby so he knew it was a big chance he could have been lying about everything he was saying.

" Damn they from the West." All them niggas do is finesse Mellow thought to himself

" well that's a good start now we know where to start looking for em." Stacks said Big B

" so what you got for me stacks I gave you a location, I think that's a damn good start considering how big st.louis is." Big Bobby said with bass in his voice.

" I got a couple stacks for you chill Big's fb B and take some of that bass out yo voice, we don't want no smoke big homie." Mellow said to Big Boddy coming to his brother defense.

" thanks cool with me, no disrespect." Big Bobby said calming himself down.

" damn Big B its like that I see", Stacks said with a sneaker " Crazy thing is I had more than a couple for you but lil bra said he got you so im a fall back."

"These bitch as niggas just really got that shit off, they don't know them Tippers 10 steps ahead of they silly ass." Big Bobby thought to himself. " aw its cool im taking whatever yall giving you know I fucks with yall we all from the same side."

"light Big B make sure you keep in touch if you find anything else out let us." Mellow said handing him the stack of money. "Oh and you can count it if you want to make sure its all der, that's just play money." And walked off

" Big Bobby my brother the one that don't trust you and just think, I really think you rubbed him the wrong way, I can't keep saving you man so make sure you let us know when you hear something." JStacks said sounding cool.

"I got yall big homie no faking. Yall can trust me, man I see yall about yall paper too." Big Bobby said tryna smooth things over. They gave a head nod and dabbed it up and went they was.

Once the brothers made it back to the truck they waited till Big B pulled off as usual. " Man Bra I am telling you we gonna have to end up knocking his ass watch that nigga is not to be trusted" Mellow said to his brother.

"Bra I know in due time I can most definitely feel the vibe." JStacks said to his brother watch Big Bobby pulling off the parking lot. " you hungry lil bra you want to grab a bite to eat real quick."

"Naw big bra I aint really hungry for no food, I want to follow this bitch ass nigga just to see what type of time he on. The shit he say justdon't sit right with me man, its like he tell us what we want to hear you know how I feel about that shit." Mellow said shaking his head watching Big B hit the corner.

" yeah they tell what you want to hear when in fear, I peed that bra believe me but how we been knowing Big B long as the paper coming he a tell you what you need to know."Jstacks said to his brother.

Mellow said real seriously, "Man bra you gotta think about that, that nigga know more that what he telling us, and Im telling you he playing both sides."

JStacks sat back and took everything his little brother was saying in and he knew he was going to have to put Big B down for playing both sides. " I see where you at Lil Bra we a give him some more time to see what he come up with, and that nigga gotta remember we know his wear abouts why he think shit sweet."

"sayless big bra I told I been lurking anyways." Mellow stated.

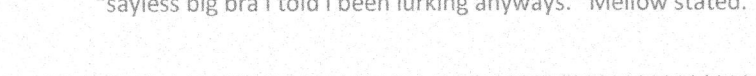

"The Brown's a put you down, yall really have to watch them niggas they sneaky as hell too." Big B said to the Bigg Tippers and SK.

"The Brown's huh, and that lil punk ass saying aint moving shit big hommie you could of saved that shit." Lil E said to Big Bobby

"Dang Bra chill on Big B, you know he don't mean us no harm, he just getting us hip," Nas said to Lil E hoping he a catch the hint to chill.

"my bad Big Bra you right that was a lil fly, but them niggas is really something man I cant stand meeting they asses. They do too much for no fucking reason they deserve everything they got coming." Big Bobby replied.

" My bad Big B but for them niggas to be so grimy the keep letting you walk away so yall got to have some kind of understand. But if the bitch ass niggas the way you say they is they more than likely gonna try to put yo ass down Big B, just think about it you know to much, and you really think niggas cool with paying you for information, I mean we don't have a choice we don't know you and you doing us a favor, they don't even respect the code you think they gonna let you off free?" Lil E said to Bobby because he clearly wasn't getting it.

"Mannn Bra fuck them niggas I can't stress that to y'all enough. they to mutherfucking heavy and they think they can't get touched. aye I know karma ain't got no time limit and I'm playing with fire, it's crazy I trust y'all more than them but, respect is everything to me with that being said, them niggas need everything they got coming to them!" Bobby said seriously letting them know he was on point.

"Well now that we all on the same page lets make something shake." SK chimed in clarifying everybody was cool.

"Yeah when the next time you post to meet with these niggas Big B we can always sit in the cut and wait for you!" Lil E asked

"It's been a min so I know they bout waiting on me to check in." Big Bobby responded

"Cool tell they ass you think you found one of the spots that a be some more leeway for you and that about get they ass off to back I know they think you playing both sides!" Nas mentioned

Sk "I like the way you think Lil Bra, you want to get on they ass when they come check the spot out...

"Naw we can't do that they ass gonna know we set em up!" Nas cut Sk off before he could even finish

"Mannn fuck all that we posted them niggas come sliding then it's like that, they better blend the fuck in or I'm lighting they asses up!" Lil E said

"I can ride with they asses and if y'all want me to that way we know mfs just peepin the seen for sure, you know the niggas ain't gonna try shit why I'm wit em they don't even trust me like that." Big Bobby said making a valid point.

"yeah you might be on to something but I think we should maybe trail they ass just in case they think you gave them enough information, I mean the raw reality of it Big B you a loose end to them and we can put shit past these niggas." Sk mentioned.

" Bet im a shoot the location where we post to meet at that way yall can just tail us from der." Big Bobby said agreeing with the plan.

"cool now we need a duck off that way its not really a spot but them niggas a think it is." Lil E said hope they knew damn well he wasn't taking about one of the stash spots.

" we need a throw off spot Bra I know where you at, we can always us the vacant build over der on westside they know that's where we from already might as well make the shit make sense." Nas stated giving Lil E a piece of mind, making it aware they both were on the same page.

"See man that's why I fucks with yall, yall ass be on it! Sk said sounding even more confident in the plan. " Yall asses got properties and shit and I aint even know it , that's the real boss shit right der how can I get on that shit that's where the real money at..."

"we can rap about all that another time big dog, right now is not a good time" Lil E had to set in and cutting the bullshit short he hated Mixing business with personal business and this was most some personal ass shit. " Big Boddy just hit us when you meeting the niggas if you want us to trail you we most definitely can before are if you want us to just trail you back to yo car and spot we can do that shit too. But these niggas gotta go and I mean quick!" Lil E was tired of all the small talk he was ready to go check in with the fam it had been damn near a month and Rah was showing any signs of improvement and niggas wasn't feeling him are his family pain and that wasn't sitting right with him. He felt his twins pain and he wanted mutherfuckers to pay. " Nas Bra give Big Boddy the address for me please I have to go check in Bra, im a meet you in the car."

"Bet Bra I'm right behind you" Nas told Lil E as he was walking off. " iight Big B just hit us up when you make your mind up you're a smart man with a plan I know." Lil E stated as he walked off dabbing Big Bobby up.

" Aw most def Big Bra, faces up I got yall soon as I get word." Big Bobby said

" iight my niggas yall C safe out here, we a bump heads in a min." Sk chimed in walking off after a quick one arm embrace.

Chapter 4

"well that's some damn good news if you ask me, she no longer need that damn machine and not to mention the tubes being gone make her look so much better." Nas stated as he got in the car with Lil E. "I don't know what I would do with out you man yall really do mean a lot to me, I can't stress that shit enough. We gonna be headed that way in a few did yall need us to bring anything?" Nas asked as he got all the way in the car.

Lil E look at Nas in shocked and asked, " who the hell yo ass lying to I told yo ass we gotta go check in at the hospital man."

"iight hold on let me put you on speaker," Nas said in a playful way.

"shut yo big head ass up he talking to me black ass dude now chill yo ass out why you try kill his game, what if I was somebody he actually like, you fucked up Bra,"

" what the hell my muther fucking bad, let me mind my business, we a see you in min sis" Lil E said laughing in disbelief.

"iight ill see yall in a min A-t had to leave s"o its just me." Niecey mentioned hoping that a make them hurry up as she hung up.

" Damn Bra so what up what the news I know its something if Niecey calling you." Lil E said as they pulled off.

" she just sent me a picture bra they took her off the breathing machine they said she breathing on her own but she still isn't responding to things." Nas replied with a sense of hope.

" so what you want to do bra, that some big news you tryna go see sis, you know I can handle this business by myself if need be." Lil E stated.

"Hell Naw Bra you know I aint leaving you out here by yourself, aint no tell what these niggas might be on when they come threw, it they fault any fucking way, I need good look at these bitch ass niggas bra." Nas said in a daze.

" iight Sk said he gonna ride with Big Bobby to the location that way if they ass try something mfs a be on game and can get out the way. He called why you was in the store Bra he said you aint answer so he called me." Lil E said filling him.

" sounds like a plan I know SK a handle what eva them niggas think they got." Nas stated.

"Well lets shoot to the Hospital until he call back." Lil E said

"Naw bra you know service trash in that place and if I go you know I aint gonna want to leave right out." Nas stated sadly.

"light big bra lets just head to the spot."

* *

"light Big B this the plan I am going to be the driver that way they know you aint by yourself and aint no tell who all you got with you. It a make the think twice about anything grimy they was planning on." Sk said to Big Bobby.

"yeah I feel you, them niggs know where my moms stay man so we gotta move careful they bitch ass sent me a picture of they lil hommies helping her in with some bags." Big Bobby said in deep thought

"we got trust me aint shit gonna happen to you are your moms lil bra." Sk said seriously. " why the hell you aint been said nothing that's mad disrespectful..."

"Man Big Bra im a handle them niggas on my own time, that shit personal." Big Bobby said shaking his head in agreement about it being disrespectful.

"you think they want beef with you are they was just sending a message, what made the niggas send a picture like they watching you, is it something you aint tell them, I mean why the fuck they playing with ya moms lil bra." Sk asked trying to make sense of everything.

" Man big bra I been telling you them niggas is just disrespectful, and honestly I don't give a fuck what I did to them at this point, that a n muther fucking way to send me no message and you beef with ghost, they aint the only ones that's been playing detective Big Bra." Big B stated insuring Sk he had some insurance on the Browns as well.

"I see where you at Lil Bra but we gonna most defiantly going to handle these niggas so you handling it on your own time is out of the question." Sk said assuring Big Bobby the situation was going to get handled.

"Dealing with these mfs you always need a plan b." Big Bobby stated.

"yeah you right Lil Bra, and now its only right I drive these niggas terrible I still cant believe they playing with moms like they aint the mfs in the wrong." Sk stated

"well we meeting at a public place but it aint really safe considering the fact its where the niggas make the most money at and its they safe zone not to mention." Big Bobby wanted to make Sk aware of the situation.

" so what you telling me Lil Bra, they checking shit as we coming in are what?" Sk asked not really understanding the point Big Bobby was making.

" No what im saying is I want to drive and if anything is to happen to me you just gotta hop over to the drive said and you a know where the niggas at. I don't trust them, and I don't want to give them any more reason not to trust me, for whatever reason they already don't." Big Bobby stated.

" i mean I can just ride with you Lil Bra and just peep they scene I aint tryna put no more pressure on you then you already got, I most definitely understand what you say." Sk said insuring Big Bobby he wasn't going to risk putting his mother into any more danger.

Big Bobby responded ,"Bet they want us to meet them right before it get to dark meaning they will want to check out the spot tonight at as well, so make sure you put the Big Tippers game, I most defiantly don't want any mix with them, when it's that time." Big Bobby mentioned to Sk.

"I got you Lil Bra I called my peoples and told them that we had to meet the Browns tonight and they might be sliding threw, so you coved on that end we just need a for sure time when they do decide to slid." Sk replied.

"Bet let me call these niggas and see what time they was thinking, make it sound interesting that way it might put a fire under they asses." Said Big Bobby

Ring Ring ring " Yo Big Bobby whats the word my dude I wasn't expecting to hear from you so soon." Jstacks said sounding surprised.

"That's because I just got word of some shit and I know yall might want me to take a ride." Big B replied

"oh really well you know where we at if you ever need to talk, just pull up when ever you ready Big B, you know we here." Jstacks said.

"Man Bra what the hell type of time you on…" You could hear Mello in the background yelling at his older brother Stacks.

"you know what Big Bra I'm in route to yall right now cuz I don't Big Bobby said sounding aggravated.

You could hear Stacks telling his lil brother to chill out and calm down. " light Big Bobby how long you think you going to be, maybe if I relay the message it a give him some kind peace of mind." Stacks said in a playful way.

"im in route as we speak so it should be about 10-15 mins if that." Big Bobby stated.

"you all about business now I see, we a see you in a few Big B." JStacks replied hanging the phone up.

Before he could get the phone back in his pocket Mellow was on his top, "why the hell would you give that opp ass nigga an open invitation to just pull up on us like he our rounds. You better tighten up you don't even know if the nigga by his self are not I bet."

"well he said he was in route due to you being so snappy he aint want you feeling no type of way, so with that being said, if he is with anybody it aint nobody we a have to worry about." Stacks replied why shooting his brother you better shut the fuck up looks.

" don't try and put that loose ass shit off on me Big Bra you tweaking." Mellow replied

"Mello use your head Lil Bra how many muther fucking times we had to meet that nigga at this damn park? Right, the nigga aint that fucking slow." Stacks said in his own defense.

"Man Bra you aint see, if he was thinking the shit you aint do nothing but clarify it for him is what im say." Mellow said

"man fuck him and who eva riding with him, we aint ducking no reck, from no muther fucking body." JStacks damn near yelled.

"Say less Big Bra I got you, if don't nobody got you and you know that, right are wrong." Mellow stated and then walked off to catch a cut.

JStacks yelled after him, "it aint even been 10 mins we still got time."

On the other end The Browns was not doing nothing but digging a them selves in a deeper whole.

"Man Big B what the fuck they know where yo momma stay and they still talking to you like a lame? If you fuck with us you fuck with us and we aint letting shit like that side around my way." Sk said in disbelief but aggression.

" Just chill they aint do shit but give conformation on where they be at, that's all I really wanted, now I can go follow niggas home and shit." Big Bobby replying nonchalantly.

"ok Lil Bra my bad I see you got a plan of your own when it come to these niggas for real, they say yall niggas is different over on this side so you would know." Sk said joking but profoundly serious.

"Im the one that said we was different on the other side, and of course I do I told you that shit with my moms is personal, lets just say it's a race to see who can smoke they asses first." Big B finally came out and said it.

"aw well say less, yall niggas aint the only ones who can play detective." Sk stated referring to Big B comment from earlier.

" you got jokes I see, but it is a good thing you going with me. them niggas be trying me every fucking time, I want to know if they gonna try to pull something. I mean it a be the first encounter we had since they sent me that picture of my fucking moms." Big Bobby said in deep thought.

" Man Big B Fuck them niggas and im standing on that shit lil bra you want me to get out with you why you rap with the niggas I will, they bout think you aint got no back up anyway that's why they keep trying you." Sk said seriously

" Naw its cool Big Bra I can handle it, they see you with me and they gonna automatically think something is up, you know that shit gonna look suspect." Big Bobby stated

"Man Lil Bra fuck these niggas you know im rocking with you regardless right or wrong. But that's up to you, however you want to play it you do know the niggas I don't, and on top of that I ain't tryna fuck up nothing you already got going." Sk stated

"Good looking Big Bra just watch my head, if anything go left somebody a know what happened to me and you know I am not call you soft but we gotta think smart about this whole situation. Them niggas see you and they gonna know whats up and most def a take us both out right after they get the needed information. I told you it's a lil personal for me now." Big Bobby said to Sk.

"I got you lil bra anything crack off im shooting niggas and making a run for it, I aint leaving you hanging them niggas aint gonna know what hit they asses when this skanless muther fucker start spitting at they silly asses."

" yeah yo ass is str8 nutty big bra and you might just have enough bullets for they ass to you gotta have two drums you don't think that's a lil to much." Big Bobby said joking

"Nawwwww you can never have to many bullets Lil Bra, that's like saying you can have to much money." Sk said look at his signature gun sitting between his legs on the flow of the truck.

"light Big Bra we gonna be pulling up in a few I got my Draco under the seat if you need it I know it's a lil smaller than what you usta to but it could come in handy." Big Bobby informed Sk.

"Goooood shit Lil Bra when I say they aint got shit coming if they try it we might be out numbered but you got my word Lil Bra I got." Sk said with some seriousness in his voice.

"light we coming up on they asses after the next two stop lights. And im parking in my usually spot it has a nice view of the whole park no faking." Big Bobby stated

"Got you Lil Bra and this right here should make it your last run in with these Clowns."
Sk said giving Big Bobby some dab.

"Hopefully Big Bra, anything changes im a call you from the burner phone." Big Bobby
said bouncing out the car.

"Well that was quick Big B." JStacks said to Big Bobby as he walked up to the normal
meet spot.

" Yeah I told you yall might want me to take a ride, I found out where the niggas be at
finally." Big Bobby stated.

"Aw really I wonder what gave you a change of heart." JStacks said being and asshole.

" Naw noo change of heart I just had to come out my pockets to get the information I
wanted, yall Bothers know how the game go." Big Bobby responded.

"I like how you handle business Big B I gotta give it to you, honestly I thought this was
going to go a whole other way." JStacks said.

" You made it clear what you wanted, when you trying to get this shit out the way man.
Im tryna be done with this whole situation all together it went to far. My moms ain't
have nothing to do with nothing." Big B said to JStacks .

" what you saying Bobby." Mellow asked Big Bobby.

"I'm saying I'm ready to be done with this whole situation, I went in my pockets just to
show y'all I ain't on no bs, I thought we was better than that honestly, no disrespect."
Big Bobby said to Mellow seriously.

" I can most decently respect that, so you gonna slide with us to show us the spot or you
just got the location?" Mellow asked

" honestly I was gonna slide the bitch showed me one of they spots, my mind a gps so
it's easier for me to show y'all I go off landmarks, I ain't good with them Lou streets." Big
Bobby said

" iight sayless you tryna slide now or you need to go park yo whip first. JStacks asked.

" I can hop in with y'all or y'all can ride with me it's up to y'all." Big Bobbie nervously.

"You can jump in with us, gone and lock up so we can head out" Mellow said.

"Cool sayless y'all want me to grab the heat at all or we just checking shit out." Big Bobby asked

"Chill Big B we cant off they ass tonight we gotta check some cuts first and see what we up against." JStacks said

"Aw well shit I can lock up from here I'm have my peoples come grab that mf." Big Bobby said.

" you on it I see Big B, who pissed you off." Mellow stated with question.

"Aye Bra that shit y'all pulled with my moms was outta line and it's not a joking matter!" Big Bobby states with anger

" what you mean Big Bobby no disrespect I'm lost on that lil situation" Mellow id convincingly

" you playing with me right?" Big Bobby asked Mellow now in somewhat of a rage.

"can we talk about this shit later so we can get this shit over, it's not sitting right with me Big Bobby!" Mellow said confused but angry.

"Aw yeah we most definitely can." Big Bobby stated.

" Let's gone head that way." Mellow replied back.

"It's about time y'all agreed on something we can take my truck cuz you niggas tripping, Big B you can ride shot gun, lil bro gone head an chill out in the back." JStacks stepped in, taking control of the situation.

" sayless big bra lets roll." Mellow said to his brother.

Walking to JStacks car Big Bobby was able to shoot SK a text "everything is a go, 5-10 gone an head on out"

"What you texting yo peoples Big Bobby?" JStacks asked noticing him in his phone.

"Yeah you think I'm leave my shit up here these y'all people no offense not mines." Big Bobby said making a valid point.

"He do got a point big bra chill" Mellow said coming to Big Bobby defense " make yo call Big Boddy we in the car."

"It's cool I told them where it was at they only like 15 mins if that." Big Boddy started.

"Aw well shit lets head them ways!" JStacks yelled.

* *

"Aye bra Sk just said it's a go." Nas whispered to Lil E after reading his text message.

It's crazy they really think I'm dumb to everything that's going on. I really hate the way I think but being my Best friend is in a comma I really don't know how to feel at this point. I know karma don't really have a time limit so I can't really justify wants already established. Everything is above me at this point. Necey thought to herself. "Hey what ya whispering about y'all know I'm nosey as hell!" Necey said getting both Lil E and Nas attention.

" Really Necey why you always do that shit if you know whats being said." Her twin Lil E asked her.

" Because we all know its not good to make assumption, I was just clarifying, you can't speak in a room of people if you don't expect for it to be heard." Necey said to her twin sarcastically.

" I like how yo big head ass put that, but you still shouldn't ear hustle that aint a good look smart ass." Lil E said back to his twin.

"Well tighten ya lips up or something and lets not act like I don't want revenge as bad as yall do."

"Aye, Necey we got this I need you to keep doing what It Is you been doing and making sure my sister know we here waiting on her to make a speedy recovery." Nas said to Necey sounding stern yet gentle.

" we need you praying for us somebody have to sis, we headed str8 bad hear once we finish." Lil E stated

" I love yall and please be safe." Necey said and walked back to Rah Rah bed side.

"lets just go Bra she got enough going on in her head she aint telling us about, give her some time." Nas said to Lil E "Love you more Necey an thanks for everything." He stated and walked out the room.

"Aye sis I love you and be expecting a call on our way back." Lil E said embracing his twin and headed out the door.

Unable to really do or say anything Necey just stood in the corner and watch as the door closed to the room. "God please watch over them only you know they path so please keep them safe. Aman." Only thing really left to do is pray its beyond me at this point. " I really do hope they aint on no silly shit." Necey thought to herself and sat at her best friends side.

****

"Damn Big Bobby these niggas really 30 mins out?" Mellow turned around in the front seat to ask.

"yeah I told yall I had to come out my pockets to get the information, the niggas like ghost. I was saying the same thing, but that only help me confirm where the niggas really be at." Big Bobby replayed.

"Damn I like the way you be thinking Big Bobby, that's some real shit." JStacks said to Big Bobby looking in his rearview mirror.

"yeah they pretty much respected too, the girl told me I was getting my self in a hole I couldn't get out of but, fuck it I see they know where my moms stay so I might as well help yall why I can, man Mellow no disrespect but I honestly thought yall sent a picture it was a lil young nigga an I just assumed it was yall that sent that picture, but that bitch had to tell so its on after to night yall do what yall gotta do but after to night I got my own business to tend to no disrespect." Big Bobby said looking out the window as they crossed the Mississippi river.

Watching Big Bobby in visor Mellow stated "yeah I can fell you on that one Big B, I aint the type to be playing with peoples moms so my word is bond Big Dog them Niggas got what ever it is coming for them."

Focused on the road JStacks knew he had crossed the line when he sent that picture , it was to late at this point he just shook his head and said " aye we coming up on Delmar should I take that all the way down to kingshighway…"

"I don't know Big Bra she just said Maple and Union. Page, and mlk run all that way from down here once we get to Union, I can tell you where we going." Big Bobby said on his toes at this point.

"Cool I know Delmar a take us to Kingshighway I had a lil thot usta stay in so apartments by a taco bell over that way." JStacks said laughing trying to brighten the move.

"Yeah it's in the area or the same Zone as they call it.." Big Bobby said sarcastically but with an attitude.

" If you want to Big B we can push on what ever out here for them Niggas playing with you moms like that, that's some disrespectful as shit, or we can find that Bitch and make her pay for playing both sides…" Mellow said before Big Bobby could finish cutting him off

" Naw im a handle my own business on my own time, y'all got enough to worry about as it is." Big Bobby said seriously.

"I can't do nothing but respect you on that note!" Mellow said to Big Bobby genuinely as ever.

"Well Big B you know we rocking with you, you stuck yo neck out for us on this one" Jstacks said backing his brother decision.

" Let's just handle this lil situation first that way I know she some what safe I know they gonna come retaliate if something happen right after they sent me that shit!" Big Bobby said with anger.

"Damn this mother fucker jumping like they in New Jack City wtf they ass think they CmB for real?" Big Bobby stated taking they mind off him and his situation.

"CMB...I huh I can see it I bet they asses got these apartments on lock!" JStacks as he checked out the seen.

"Yeah they most def making some moves over these ways. We need to make it back over here and quick, if they got Big B info it's only a matter of time before they get anything on us!" Mellow said with supination.

"I gotta piss I'm about to stop at Walgreens."JStacks said pulling in to the parking lot.

"Really Bra ya timing really couldn't be any worst at this point." Big Bobby said some what frustrated.

"We need to drive back by that way anyway y'all just watch my headache and let me know, if anybody come or got that way." JStacks said hopping out the truck.

"Excuse my brother Big B apparently he can't hold his batter." Mellow said coming to his big brother defense.

"Yeah I see." Big Bobby said aggravated.

"Well slid behind the driver set so you can watch that walk way" Mellow said changing the subject.

As JStacks walked in the store he noticed he had a missed called from who he sent to help Big Bobby Moms. "What's wrong lil bra everything good?!" He said once the other end answered.

"Aye you knew dude had somebody in his truck, mfs never pulled up but it pulled off and I know niggas ain't making enough money to drive magical cars!" He yelled one the phone

"Huh he told us they sent everything but I guess he ain't really trusting nobody or he playing both sides." JStacks said.

"Well I damn sure ain't trusting his fat ass!"

"He did say he was gonna text his people but made it like they was close by. Throw everything away and I'm a do the same at Walgreens now!" Jstacks said in reference to the phones they did business on.

Back in the truck Big Bobby shot a text of the truck color and they location in case anything took place to Nas.

"What the hell taking his ass so damn long!" Mellow asked now getting a bit frustrated.

" Mannnnnn that's yo brother you better go check on him and make sure he ain't fall in." Big Bobby said jokingly.

"Is it me or did everybody that went in after him came out." Mellow said suspiciously.

"You want me to go check on I know I'm security and all but didn't he say he just had to us the bathroom." Big Bobby stated.

"Yeah let me go see what this nigga doing!"

Just as Mellow was reaching for the door Big Bobby stopped him. " Hold tight, It's like a couple guys walking from them apartments and it look like they headed this way."

"Ohhhh shit let me call this nigga" Mellow said letting the door handle go and pulling his phone out.

Still in line now at the register Jstacks answered as the guys walked in

"Head out now needed some business phone the fat fucker might be tryna play us." Jstacks said as he grab the bag and walked out not worried about the 3 men walking in.

Mellow hung up the phone as he seen his brother coming out the store and all 3 men looking his way as he made the comment. "He on his way out now Big B." Mellow said now thinking.

"I can see that, but did you get a look at the 2 guys in the back!" Big Bobby said now amp.

"Yeah I did them the Niggas we looking for!" Mellow said making it like he was on his toes.

" Aint this bout a bitch!" Big Bobby stated sounding in disbelief.

Jstacks heard Big Bobby as he was getting in the truck, " damn wtf I miss?"

Before Mellow could even respond Bobby said " you mean to tell me you and see them 3 niggas walk in that store and mug yo ass!"

"Yeah Big Bra I was tryna put you on game but you said you was already headed out." Mellow respond and shook his head.

"Fuck all that we both saying it was them niggas!" Big Bobby said applying pressure.

"We can sit and watch see how shit play and switch whips and come back." JStacks mentioned feeling like a dumb ass for sleep in the opp Territory.

"Sounds like a plan to me Big Bra, I ain't got shit else planned." Mellow responded, tryna see where Big Bobby head was at considering what his brother just told him.

"Yo Truck cool Big Bobby or you had other plans?" JStacks turned around and asked.

" My truck better be cool, and if y'all want me to come back I will I need to make sure these niggas dead dead." Big Bobby told the Brown Brothers.

"You don't need to check in with nobody or nothing Big B." JStacks asked him

"Why you so worried about my damn truck and these niggas right here in yo mfn face!" Big Boddy said defensive and Stern.

"I'm just tryna make sure everything good on your end." Jstacks replied.

"Well pay more attention to the situation at hand the niggas coming back out." Big Bobby said nodding his head in the direction of the entrance door.

"Yeah that's most definitely them." Mellow said looking hard.

Turning around he noticed the guys looking the way of the truck but keeping it moving. "Why they looking like they know we in here?" JStacks questioned.

"Yeah they is looking hard as a muther fucker, you a think they can see threw the 5%!" Big Bobby stated.

"Maybe it's just a unknown car in the Zone, and they tryna check shit out maybe we should head on out and just side back." Mellow said making a valid point.

" you right Lil Bra we can head back them ways but I need to hit a few corners first!" Jstacks said.

"I see I ain't the only one that peeped the street was a one way." Big Bobby said sarcasticallY, hitting he was on the same page.

" Make it like we noticed them, they asses ain't moving shit!" Mellow replayed making it known he wanted smoke.

"We a put the lot ass down they try something!" Jstacks said as he stepped on the breaks and gas s'n off leaving a trail of smoke from Union until Arlington.

After hitting a few corners on the west side the ride back to the east was up in the air. Mellow was steady thinking on the conversation him and his brother had before the opps came in the store. It was a lot that didn't sit right with him including the fact Big Bobby didn't know who sent the picture of his moms which meant he had to playing both sides.

"The street a one way so that Mean we a have to come from the alley way in the back." Big Bobby said breaking the silence.

" we on the same type of time Big B! Great minds really do think a like." Mellow responded

"We ain't even made it to the bridge yet an y'all asses already on it!" Jstacks mentioned.

"Can you stop at a Quick trip I need to get my shit together?" Big Bobby asked

"Why Quick Trip Big Bobby?" Jstacks asked already know why

"I'm fat and I'm hungry! Y'all ever try the Doritos chips with the chill and cheese? And y'all know they got the taquitos ready to eat! Quit playing with a Hood Nigga!" Big Bobby said honestly.

Mellow googled the closest Quick Trip and they pulled in. Big Bobby hopped out the back and head str8 to the chips. Mellow watch him to make sure he wasn't on no slick shit.

"We gonna have to kill this nigga." JStacks said watching as well

"Welp let me get my ass in the back!" Mellow said already on game.

Walking to the register Big Bobby noticed Mellow hopping in the back seat. He know something was up so why paying for his stuff he shot Sk a text " watch they head, we headed back them ways later." Hopping in the front seat Big Bobby already knew what was going on. " what you got sleepy or something Lil Bra, gotta stretch out before the next mission?" He asked.

"Yeah I like to rest my eyes first." Mellow said sarcastically.

" Let him think Big B, it's good for the both of us."JStacks replied.

"Let me do the same." Big Bobby replied .

"Naw I wanted to rap with you first." Stacks replied

"What's the word?" Big B asked

"Yo truck, did you ever check on it?" Stacks asked

"Naw, but it should be at my moms crib." Big Bobby stated already prepared.

Come up on the bridge Jstacks knew it was now or never. " you know it moved right, and nobody never pulled up."

" Yeah I had my moms with me and she might have gotten scared once she seen the nigga in the picture with her, did she ever make it back?" Big Bobby questioned being Sk never replied back.

Before Jstacks could reply Mellow sat up and shot once point blank range with his 40 no questions asked.

" what the fuck was that lil bra?" Stacks asked catching the wheel and pulling over.

" you see any cars?" Mellow asked

" No." Stacks replied

"Turn ya hazard lights on, you gonna have to buy some new weights." Mellow said

" No need to ask if you seen the damn rope!" JStacks yelled jumping out headed to the trunk as Mellow grab the weights at his feet jumping out with his brother.

"Damn why this nigga gotta be so damn big?" Mellow said out loud as he dragged Big Bobby feet and checking his pockets only thing he found was the phone.

"Damn the nigga fat and broke what he spent his last at the gas station or what!" JStacks questioned.

"Just lift on 3 ain't no cars came in a min." Mellow said looking around before getting in position grab Big Bobby off the ground.

"I'm gonna have to get more weights." Jstacks replied as he tied the las weight to the rope getting in position.

One two three! They rolled Big Bobby over just as a car passed slowing down being good samaritans.

"Just get in Bra and quick!" Mellow said jumping in the passenger seat.

Before Mellow even finished his sentence Jstacks shot around to the driver side and hoped in honking at the car as they drove past.

"Damn you strategize quick, you ready to tell me what the hell you just came up with!" JStacks asked his younger brother.

"You don't like being left out the loop now do you? When the duck was you gonna tell me you had mfs go to that man momma house? I told yo ass that shit was a dumb ass idea!" Mellow replied.

"That don't mean just go killings people now do it." Stacks snapped back.

"Funny thing is I remember tell you the same thing when you wanted to just go shooting at females!"Mellow snared and looking at his brother.

" Fuck you Mel!" Stacks replied knowing his actions was the reason for everything.

"Right now it's fuck me, he knew I ain't know about the picture and you forced my hand when you made the truck comment, whats done is done!" Mellow replied looking out the window.

****

"Aye bra did you ever hear back from Sk or Big Bobby at all?" Lil E asked Nas.

"Naw I ain't heard nothing since that text Big B sent earlier." Nas responded checking his phone just in case he did miss a call.

" Man something don't feel right, call Sk he would have been checked in." Lil E said.

RING RING RING RING

"What's the word Lil Bra is everything everything." Sk asked when answering the phone.

"What the hell is going on, why you ain't checked in you ain't heard nothing from Big B he was with them niggas and we ain't heard nothing." Nas said all at once.

"I been down the street from his moms he texted me and told me to tell y'all they was headed back but he ain't say shit else." Sk said watching in Big Bobby's truck.

"Well why the hell you ain't said shit!" Nas questioned

" Cuz man they had mfs following me they just pulled off I was giving it sometime."Sk said still checking his surroundings.

"Head back this way we need to rap, Lil E got a feeling and them ain't nva good." Nas replied and hung up

Sk pulled off slowly shaking his head at the thought of Big Bobby getting killed.

"They followed Sk after Big Bobby got in, he told Sk to put us on game but he could cuz mfs was watching him. He headed back now Big Bobby said they was coming back but he ain't heard nothing else." Nas told Lil E.

"Damn Big B, he was a real nigga, if Sk cool it gotta be him." Lil E replied on disbelief.

"You think they really killed him Lil E?" Nas aske.

"He a loss end to them, they got the information they needed and then it's the if they found out he was playing both side." Lil E replied making a very valid point.

"We a speak on it more when Sk get here, right now we gotta watch out heads in cause they tryna catch another body tonight." Nas said.

"They asses ain't coming back that's to much killing in one night." Lil E replied.

"I guess you an expert on that kind of shit?" Nas asked sarcastically.

" Naw that feeling came out the blue is why I say that." Lil E replied honestly.

" well say that then." Nas said.

After a good 15-20 mins Sk finally pulled up.

"Damn you sure you came from the Eastside?" Lil E asked.

"Hell yeah im 15 mins from everywhere." Sk said amp.

"I see." Lil E replied.

"Man what's going on with Big Bobby ?" Nas asked.

"He ain't answering his phone and I got his damn truck." Sk said now worried.

"I told you." Lil E said shaking his head

"What you mean Lil E." Sk asked already knowing but wanting him to go deeper in details.

"He sent Nas a text of the Walgreen and the color of the whip they was in." Said Lil E.

"Yeahhhhh and dude was talking shit on his way out when we went in!" Nas yelled mad he over looked that whole situation.

"Nowwwwww you see what the fuck I'm saying!" Lil E replied hitting Nas on his shoulder.

"Man them niggas gotta go! They sent Big B a picture of his moms basically saying they know where she stay!" Sk said with intensity.

"That's some fucked up shit, that must be why they pulled off from his moms spot." Nas stated.

"Them mfs wicked! They ain't respecting shit they ain't have to bring Big B moms in this shit. I'm with you when you right Sk and them mfs gotta go!" Lil E replied.

"Yeah that's some cold-hearted shit I guess shooting at females wasn't good enough." Nas replied.

" Man fuck them and I cant said that shit enough, fuck em fuck em fuck." Sk said furious.

" Good thing you know where his moms stay SK we gonna have to start checking in with her." Lil E mention.

" Yeah but you don't think its gonna seem suspect we just start showing up out of the blue." Nas questioned being no one has yet to report anything.

" we a just have to give it time, we can all go and make it like we haven't heard from him and we was checking to see if she heard anything." Sk stated, knowing that a give them all a chance to meet her and reasons to check in.

" Yeah that way we can all introduce ourselves." Nas chimed in letting Sk know everybody was on the same page.

" On God and she a have a chance to properly meet us, hopefully she can tell something about the mfs who helped her." Lil mentioned.

" See I like that we all on the same page cuz right now im in a rage." Sk stated.

" He risked his life for my sister I cant do nothing but respect for that he aint have to do all that shit for us man and im talking before the picture shit. He still knew the risk Long Live My Nigga Big B, you will live threw me!" Nas stated with passion.

Meanwhile back at the hospital things seem to take a turn for the worst for Rah-Rah. She had to go back on the breathing matchin. This just only made matters worst. More rage more frustration Niecy didn't know if she should call and give the update or just keep on with her own plan, things where already going as planned. To her surprise they already owned a lot of property she was looking to invest in, being she didn't believe in coincidences she knew it was in her best inters to just go with the flow. Know it was enough going on she did not want to add fire to the flame. She watched as they put her sister back on life support and continued to plan. "I promise I got you Rah just keep fighting you know you a fighter." Niecy said out load. She sat at her sister side and held her hand.

CHAPTER 5

" So you really mean to tell me that truck just pulled up to his moms spot and aint nobody get out?" Mellow questioned his brother and the Lil Homie Trey.

" He made it like his moms was with him Mel, so maybe he was just tryna cover his peoples ass." Jstacks said.

" Nawwww wasn't no old lady driving that truck and the only reason mf aint get they ass out is because they knew we was on they ass." Trey said with meaning.

" yeah he was most def tryna cover his ass and his ass was playing both sides. " Mellow said siding with his brother.

" I just sat and watch, once yall said that was done I shook out I cant hurt no old ladies Big Bra I cant even fake it." Trey said honestly.

" Yeah I can most def feel you on that shit Lil Bra." Mellow said shoot his older brother a look.

" I really did appreciate that Lil Bra, and like I said no harm no fow and we wasn't on no disrespectful shit we just needed to send a message." Jstacks replied looking both his Lil Brother and Trey in the face.

" yeah that was most def just a message lil bra but he aint take it that way so we had to handle that for you I mean he seen your face and everything we went threw his phone and found out his ass was playing both sides after all. We wasn't gonna do shit to his moms but he made it clear he aint know if it was us or they asses that took the picture and he wasn't letting up until he found out." Lil E said coving for his brother even doe he was left out the loop on everything.

"Long as you played it smart Big Bra I know yall gonna all do what it is you gotta do. that sound like some more unnecessary ass beef if you ask me." Trey responded.

"Part of the main reason he sleeping where he sleeping." JStacks responded already knowing he was gonna take Big Bobby out but not at the moment his brother did.

"Well long as we all on the same page of leave his moms alone im cool, I can't do that to no old ladies I know I might sound weak but we all gotta stand for something ya know." Trey said making sure they knew he wasn't the one for the job if it had to be done.

"Believe me lil bra I understand where you coming from, we aint that damn ruthless to that to a old lady." Mellow replied to his comment insulted.

" No disrespect but The Browns will put you down, and some times being ruthless gets you what you want." The Lil Homie Trey responded.

" See I like the way you think Trey. And believe me when I say its no disrespect taking." JStacks said to lighten up the mood.

" Now that we all on the same page, what we gonna do about these CMB niggas they asses making some moves over that way." Mellow said bring the focus back to the problem at hand.

"What you tryna do take it over after we take them out?" Trey asked now all ears being it was money involved.

" Damn Trey I like the way yo ass think lil bra. We can most def make that happen but first we need make a trip back across the water to see these niggas in day light." Jstacks responded.

" Bet we need to make that happen like now then." Mellow chimed in.

"light we can take my truck." Jstacks said

"you sure you want to take your truck again Bra we was in yo shit last time you know." Mellow questioned his brother.

"Fuck them Niggas you know how many Tahoe's it is with Illinois plates?" Jstacks said sarcastically.

" come on now Big Bra you know yo truck noticeable with them damn 28's." Trey replied seriously on the same page as Mellow.

"Man fuck them, I want them to know I'm on they ass and I'm coming for them." Jstacks yelled.

"Nigga it just aint gonna be yo ass in the car now is it?" Mellow snared being his brother was missing the point of playing it smart and not tough.

"Yall acting straight noid. They gonna be watch whatever pull up if you ask me and we aint pulling up we just going to hit a few corners." Jstacks said honestly just wanting to see the area in day light.

" Fuck it, we can slide I got my heat with me." Trey replied clutching on his glock.

"welp I cant let you two hot heads ride with out me somebody gonna have to calm yall down." Mellow replied shaking his head.

****

"Man you still aint heard nothing from Niecy." Nas asked Lil E after hanging up from calling her.

"she bout got yo ass blocked, I can't believe how open she got you. Bra out of all the girls in the world you want Niece, never would I have ever guessed it." Lil E said to Nas avoiding his question as Nas went to dail her number again.

"for real bra its to much shit going on for her not to be answering her damn phone, call her ass and see where the fuck she at E and I aint playing." Nas replied

"You know she bout at the hospital Bra she don't even get signals in der all the time just chill." Lil E said

" Nawwww its like you avoid her for some reason and she avoid me, something up fuck it im going to the hospital, I need to check on my sister." Nas said making shit make sense.

"Let's go I think that's what she tryna tell us something up so come see whats up." Lil E replied seriously heading to the truck.

"Aye watch that truck E." Nas Said as the Truck with Illions plates, tints, and rims pasted by.

"where the fuck them Niggas come from, and I want to know if they seen us or if they headed to the dummy spot." Lil E replied.

" Naw if they seen us I think they would have stop and remind you we really cant say if dude remember our faces or not they gotta be headed to the dummy spot." Nas mentioned.

"Them Niggas hitting corners I see, trust me. We need to make a trip. Sk know something like where them niggas stay." Lil E said eyeing the Truck as it hit the corner.

"Lets head to the hospital, they ass gonna be mad when they get down der and they see it's a deads man land mfs come where eva we stand." Nas replied hoping in the truck.

"aye you think Niecy know about the properties we brought for her and Rah-Rah." Lil E said tryna change the subject.

"What makes you say that?" Nas questioned known he aint said nothing.

"she smart but nosey as hell, I remember when we was little we couldn't even have surprise birthdays because she always found shit out before hand." Lil E said smiling.

"she really is beauty, brains and insane." Nas stated with a lil laugh.

"We should tell her, Rah-Rah off the machines it mean great things." Lil E said easing the moment.

"Yeah that's if her ass don't already know you know she has nothing but time on her hands why she been sitting up here aint no telling what her ass came across. She always seem to be ahead of the game. Its crazy she put off law school for us." Nas mentioned.

"Man her ass always tryna do the right thing like she Spike Lee Lil sista. I know she the good twin because im the one who bring all the hell." Lil E replied laughing, thinking about his sister and her good heart, knowing she didn't want to be apart from her family is the reason she decided to stay.

"Tell her ass she Lil E not Spike Lee sista she know what the fuck going on, no matter how hard we tried to keep they asses away from the streets they always found out what was going on." Nas said shaking his head at the thought of them popping up in parks and clubs they should have never been at.

"Man when I said Sherlock Homies aint got shit on them." Lil E replied damn near in tears from laughter.

"She the right ones to handle this kind of shit, you know they really can make a difference with it. I love the fact she love others more she never think about herself first only the ones she loves." Nas stated with meaning.

"Bra you know you have my wishes to marry her, you get all deep and shit when you speak of her and I aint usta to that kind of shit from you." Lil E said with groused out and confused face.

"I will one day, first I gotta tell her I love her." Nas said shaking his head trying to figure out how he was going to tell her after all these years he wanted to be with her for the rest of his life.

"What the hell Bra you slacking, she bout think you like her the way I like Rah-Rah, you should have been said something. I been telling yo ass if I gotta see my sister with any nigga why the hell wouldn't it be you." Lil E said jabbing Nas in the arm.

"Man Bra if I found out about her having a boyfriend she would of hated me. I promise she would of never looked at me the same." Nas said smiling thinking about how jealous he would have been seeing her with another man.

"You should have been made that move, her ass don't even look at niggas the same being what the hell I tell her. She ask me for advise and all the niggas be after her for Is her looks and her bag. They cant stand her ass because of me." Lil E replied proudly.

"She different I can give you that." Nas said giving Lil E a dab.

"you welcome my boy, just don't say I aint tell you she was crazy." Lil E said returning the dab.

When Nas and Lil E finally made it to the hospital everything wasn't everything and they didn't know who to start asking question being Niece was no where to be found. Look at Rah-Rah back on the machines really crushed they dreams.

"Hey I see you guys finally made it." Niece said sarcastically as she came back in the room with some food from the cafeteria.

"why the hell you cant answer your phone man and why you aint tell us Rah was back on the machines, Niece." Nas asked sounding very concerned.

"yall be having enough going on, trust me when I say I aint want to worry you all no more than what yall got going on." Niece snapped back

"Really Niecey what the hell you talking about? We post to all be in this shit together." Lil E stepped in.

"when the hell was yall going to tell me about the damn real-estate. I been running around like a chicken with my head cut off trying to find locations and this whole time yall had the one I wanted." Niecey snared.

" I told you she knew Bra." Lil E said looking at Nas

"That's why you aint tell us about Rah-Rah because of some real-estate?" Nas questioned Niecey

"Hell naw I aint tell yall about Rah-Rah because that wasn't going to do anything but add more fuel to the fire. I aint that damn selfish muther fuckers and Lil E you know you cant keep no secrets from me." Niece responded honestly.

"I love you Eunice." Nas finally said.

"whats with the government name?" Niece asked knowing she hated to be called that.

"I love you Niece, like I want to spend the rest of my life make you my wife type of love." Nas said with lots of passion.

"where and the hell all this coming from?" Niece asked shocked but flattered.

"wait this man just damn near proposed to you and the only thing you can say is where is it coming from, damn bra my bad I underestimate her." Lil E chimed in.

"no disrespect Nas, but you really caught me off guard but being you have my brother best wishes, I'm glad you finally decided to me. I love you too Nas believe it or not I always had a crush on you." Niece replied looking Nas in his eyes.

"You always been mines, little do you know. No crushing." Nas replied leaning in and kissing her for the first time. You could feel the chemistry between the two through out the room. They sent sparks down each other's spins and made harts skip beats.

"iight now muther fuckers that's enough already, go get a room or something. I aint tryna see all that shit until the wedding." Lil E said playing like he was cleaning his chest.

"Twin shut the hell up, you can really fuck up a wet dream you know that." Niece said rolling her eyes and laughing.

"Nigga you told me to shoot my shot so stop." Nas said laughing shaking his head.

"well now that we got that out the way, we was buying the real estate for you and Rah-Rah. Honestly it was something we had been thinking about and we was going to tell yall the night at the club but, here we are." Lil E said throwing his hands in the air

"It was supposed to be a surprise, just to see what all yall could really do, we really do believe in you." Nas said looking Niece deeply in her eyes.

"well how much did yall really believe because it a lot of things yall got hands on that I didn't know about." Niece said snapping.

"Damn Twin what the hell you been looking for, yo ass aint even got no damn money I know working part time jobs aintget your savings that fat." Lil E said to his sister now wanting to know what all she knew.

"Just know I know enough and you was funding me and Nas was funding Rah me and her had already talked and thought about it. Yall asses cant tell us no if we doing something for the greater good, making money, oh and lets not forget turning ya dirty money clean." Niece responded honestly.

"See that's why I love you, I swear its so much more but I love you girl." Nas responded with the biggest smile on his face.

"That shit aint funny why you smiling, she sick bra who the hell thinks like that." Lil E replied shaking his head with his hand on it like it was hurting.

"Just know we got enough for you to do what ever it is you want to do." Nas said now laughing.

"its a lot her ass want to do, and that's not including to you. But we cant let this situation with Rah-Rah slide. I see you can handle business why still being by her side we should have been said something to you. Its just been so much going on I didn't want to distract you from anything. And why you aint been said nothing to me, why you always do that shit." Lil E stated.

"I just want us to make our mark, we need to turn the hood clean again. We need places for women with kids to go. We need more of everything in our community. If they wont help us get where we need to be then leave it to Niece. I need something to keep my mind off the bullshit you know I leave all of that up to you, but lately I been have so many evil thoughts it cause me to go into over drive." She replied.

"What you mean." Nas and Lil E said at the same time.

"wellbeing im doing something for the greater good it causes me to think positively, and yall asses gave me a lot of free time to think some evil ass shit." Replied Niece.

"You just angry that's it that's all." Nas said.

"Naw its more to it than that, her being in here like this not right it wasn't for her she was innocent, and they didn't even care." Niece said in tears shaking her head.

Embracing her Nas hugged her tight and whisper in her ear "let it out its ok to feel how you feeling I promise it is, I been feeling the same way."

Watching the room Lil E just sat back and observed everything. Thinking to his self about the next move they would make being Rah-Rah was back on the machines and Niece knew everything. "Not trying to interrupt but I'm a head back to the truck if you want Nas you can sit up here with them for a min and I can swing back to grab you." Lil E said getting out of the chair next to Rah-Rah bed.

"What makes you think you interrupting something?" Niece said drying her eyes and pulling her head from Nas chest.

"I mean if you need a min to yourself bra go a head im a take her down to get some fresh air." Nas replied

"Bet im a head down them ways and head back I need to hit a few corners if you catch my drift." Lil E mentioned.

"just fuck what I be taking about I see." Niece chimed in rolling her eyes.

"if you aint talking business you don't be making sense twin you know it aint nothing like that." Lil E said giving his sister a playful head rub laughing.

"nigga you fucking up my leave out, doing to damn much." Niece yelling pulling away fixing her hair with her hand.

"come on let's walk him down to the truck." Nas said laughing walking out the room.

"its good to see you laughing bra real talk its been a min." Lil E side to Nas with a head nod.

" Mannnn I know you aint bout to do start this shit in these people hospital." Niece said turning in a complete cercle to make sure his ass was not crying.

"Im just saying yall really do look good together, it's a glow ya know." Lil E said throwing his hands up in the air.

"Tell me something." Niece said giggling.

****

"aye Big bra how long you plan on being over these ways?" Trey asked from the back set.
"Man as long as we have to be, I aint no damn dummy and I know what the fuck we seen."Jstacks replied frustrated.

"I mean we need to pick a stop and post for a min we cant keep driving around making shit hot." Mellow said looking over his shoulder for the thousand time.

"yall asses making me nervous I need yall to really chill google the nearest Metrolink station or we can grab a bite to eat and post up der for a min." Jstacks said.

"Now you talking I swear a nigga back here starving." Trey replied sitting up from the back seat rubbing his stomach.

"what the hell, yall niggas really thinking about food right now. Big Bobby got one off on us and he dead. we don't know shit about these niggas, who to say one of them niggas wasn't the one in the truck with him. Think about it, did you even see mfs get out that mfs when you followed it back to his moms house, that could of just been mfs make sure she was safe. He was stressing the shit with his moms that what made me blow his ass." Mellow said looking out the window in mid thought.

"so you mean to tell me you knew it was a chance he was setting us up and you just kill his ass with no remorse?" Trey asked from the back seat now confused and being he never really did see anybody get out the truck, he told his self to light that bitch up.

"I kilt his ass because he was playing both sides and it wasn't any point in getting him any deeper in the shit than he already was. He picked his side when he pulled up to the park, he wanted that to be the last time meeting with us, so I made the last time meeting with us." Mellow replied shrugging his solders.

"Long as the shit make sense that's all that matters to me." Jstacks chimed in to let Trey know Mellow never made a selfish move.

"you think it start cracking around a certain time or something Big bra is that why we waiting it out? Oh, and it's a Taco bell and Lee's by the Delmar Loop Metrolink Station." Trey replied changing the subject.

"Either or is cool with me." Jstacks replied.

"I swear you the one driving." Mellow said laughing looking at his brother shaking his head looking back out the window he noticed the metrolink station and said. "aw yeah that Metrolink shit dead, check them out."

"police city I see they asses hot down here on this end." Jstacks replied with a lil laugh looking out the window.

"Yeah guess we parking where we eat." Trey said shaking his head.

They pulled into the Lee's line not even noticing who was behind them

****

Lil E couldn't believe who he was seeing. Just as he let his window down and was about to fuck some shit up he seen a mobile truck. "damn these muther fucking niggas luck. They really think they out here lurking and they sleeping like some fucking babies. They really need to take they asses back across the water." Lil E thought to himself. He pulled out his phone and called Sk being he just left Nas and Niece at the hospital he knew he had to handle some shit by alone his brother had enough going on. "Guess who the fuck I see and the muther fuckers don't even see me!" Lil E said Laughing into the phone.

" Never did them Niggas have the balls to bring they asses back across the water!" Sk yelled into the phone.

"Oh my brother but they did, I sitting in fucking Lee's line behind they ass, guess all black people really do love chicken huh?" Lil E said sarcastically letting him know something was up.

" shit must be all bad, what you thinking and where that nigga Nas at, talk to me lil bra." Sk replied catch his vibe.

"Man I was bout to fuck they ass up and a fuck Mobile truck rode past, im bout to try and follow they ass. Or we need to hit that spot Big B took you to. Oh and Nas ass finally told Niece how he was feel I let his ass at the hospital was coming to get something to eat." Said Lil E

"iight sayless lil bra we gotta get off these phones, im a meet you at the hospital. Call me when you make if I don't beat you." Sk replied

"Bet faces up Big Bra." Lil E replied

"Faces up lil bra see you a few." Sk said and hung up.

These bitch ass niggas really think shit sweet then a come back in the same whip they want us to know its they ass. Lil E said out loud to his self, so it made more sense. He let them order they food and just grab a large sweet tea with lemon. He lost his appetite after not being able to give his opps what they came all this way looking for.

Once they made it back to the hospital Sk told Lil E to jump in with him so he could get the word. Lil E could not even get his foot in the door good enough before he started going back on his rant.

"Lil Bra just chill we going to head back them ways first and see if they really silly or just bold, either way we need to post up to day." Sk finally stopped him.

" Man lets go you want to grab Nas or did you talk to him already." Lil E said all in on breath.

" I talked to him I aint really say to much he said your sister had some runs to make so he was spending some time with Rah Rah by his self." Sk said seriously already keeping the situation in play in mind.

"true aint no need to make him feel no worst than he already do." Lil E replied nodding his head in agreement he all ready knew what that meant it was time he got they lick back.

" come on we can take my car, we already in and its tented so why the fuck not." Sk said with a lil laugh.

"Bet I got the tech lets ride." Lil E said rubbing his hands.

Coming down the forest park expressway seem like it took no time Sk was cold with the wheel and the 300 ss really did ride. Lil E had been gone for about 15 mins if that and coming up on the Lee's he seen the truck still sitting. " yeah these niggas just bold they still up here just sitting." Lil E replied nodding to the truck in the parking lot.

Sk pulled into the taco bell lot next door as if he was getting in line as he did he notice the truck finally leaving. And turned around to follow them. "Yeah im on they ass now they fucked up bring they ass back over here. Now they just look for shit." SK said making sure to stay a car behind.

"why it look like these niggas heading back to the zone is my question they really tryna catch some reck I see, the first red light you get threw they is too." Lil E agreed with anger.

"sayless lil bra I got that wheel as you can see you need to shoot too I will." Sk said to the statement just made.

"Aw naw I got you Big Bra trust me, stop so I can hope out no faking." Lil E said with so many intentions running in his head.

"yeah I got you hop in the back im a pull up on the side of they ass and that way you aint gotta get out." Sk said trying to talk some sense in Lil E.

" I just aint tryna make yo car hot no faking." Lil E replied honestly

"Lil bra fuck these plates do what the fuck you gotta do." Sk said respecting where Lil E was coming from.

Now coming up on page and Hamilton they finally caught them sleep at a red light. Lil E check for the cops and they was coming to the stop and let the window down. He help his teck 9 out the window and just let it blow as sk rode past. He noticed the car started to turn before he could really get up on them guess they really wasn't silly after all.

" damn them niggas was watch us" Sk said as he had to keep straight and took a left on to the street Goodfellow.

" Bra why I was just think the same thing." Lil E said the back seat shaking his head mad at his self for possibly missing a kill.

" Aw naw you most definitely hit something." Sk said watching in front of him. " Look Bingo he said as they came up on Martin Luther King and Goodfellow the was floating right past. " im on they ass." Sk said hitting the gas swerving around the cars in front of him.

Now coming back up on the truck Lil E let his window down and this time he made sure he didn't stop until they recked. Look out the window he notice the drive door open but no one got out.

" damn we cant even hit the block after all that action. We gonna head to my spot and I can switch cars and drop you off or I you can have Nas pull up." Sk said heading back to the highway to head home.

" that should be cool its bout to be hot as a mf out here. And I aint tryna be walking."

Surprising they made it back to the highway and was off the west in no time laughing about how the opps thought they was going to get some shit off.

****

"Who the fuck was that and how the fuck did they get up on us like that." Mellow question going in and out of conscience. He looked in the back seat and could not do nothing shake his head.

Jumping out the truck and running around to his brother side to get his heat he could hear the police sirines in coming, grabbing the guns he ran to an alley and tucked them under a trash can and shot back across the street to his truck.

How the fuck am I going to get us out of this one JStacks was thinking to himself. When he made it back to the front of the truck the police was down the street he ran to his brother side in the front seat was in disbelief.

" yall gotta hang tight do yall hear me everything going to be oh right, mistaking identity do yall hear me." JStacks said holding Mellow hand looking in the back seat.

Jstacks watched as they rushed his brothers away in the ambulance, toning out the police as they tried to take his statement. He played dumb of course, made it like they was just in the cross fire and not the target cuz he most def wanted his lick back.

****

Back at the hospital Nas was starting to get worried, it had been a min since he last heard from Niece. He knew she had to handle, and just as he was hitting redial Lil E and Niece came strolling in the room as if nothing was going on.

" Good to know yall good." Nas stated.

"thanks but I don't do hospitals and we need to go." Lil E Said to Nas Catching his vibe.

"I love yall and please be safe." Niece replied.

" I love you more Baby, im a go grab a but to eat, you want anything why im out?" Nas asked

" What ever you get is cool with me." Niece replied making it known she was ready for a bite to eat.

" Say less I see where we at, I love you Niece, I love you baby girl he said as he kissed his sister on the forehead ." Nas replied knowing he needed to rap with Lil E at this point.

" I love yall be safe please." Niece replied knowing Nas was feeling some type of way.

" love you more my love." Nas replied walking over to give her a huge and kiss.

" love you big head." Lil E replied as him and Nas walked out the door.

Before Nas said anything, he made sure they was in the car and out the way. As they made they right on to Kingshighway he finally asked his question

"What the hell just happened." Nas said seriously looking out the window knowing they was in the clear.

" we got our lick back and some." Lil E said calmly

" With out me, that shit must have been sweet." Nas said getting amp.

"Man Bra it took a few times but we hit something. Them mother fuckers brought they asses over here and it got handed to em." Lil E said really intense

" what you mean by a few times and why you keep say we?" Nas questioned.

" Me and Sk who else, you know we the only two going to ride for you." Lil E said rubbing his hand together to getting ready to tell him how everything played out.

" Aw shit I been listening let be shut the fuck so I hear this shit, go head lil bra." Nas said amp but serious as hell.

Lil E started shaking his head because he knew Nas was his driver and he was serious when he wanted to know how the store went. " Bra I caught they asses sleeping at Lee's, they bold as fuck to come back over here look for smoke, that shit was fucking with me and being you was at the hospital with Niece and Rah-Rah I couldn't let that shit fly. We pulled up to the hospital and switched cars. We got up on they ass and they seen us coming but we bumped into they ass again, they silly asses crashed out." Lil E said laughing at the tough of the situation.

" Now you know if you had yo driver that second time would not have been caused for. But less you redeemed yourself." Nas said now knowing why Sk called and played 20 questions.

" Man Bra the shit was sick Niece had to come get from Sk Spot cuz it was so hot, he aint even want to switch whips shit he had me do the who demo out his shit." Lil E mentioned.

" yeah I still need to catch reck Sk need to take us over der so we can make sure mother fuckers don't bring they asses back." Nas with rage in his voice.

" I like the way you think my brother, I was sholl saying the same thing." Lil E replied with a laugh.

" yeah you know great minds think a lot, now what you tryna eat cuz Niece ass gonna kill me if I take to long." Nas said shaking his head.

" Damn she got you like that already, go back to Lee's that shit brought my appetite back but head to the one on Kingshighway. Lil E requested.

" light I think we got problems bra, who the fuck celebrate a killing with chicken." Nas said trying to keep a straight face, but couldn't keep the laughter in.

" Aye it got to be the west in us I don't know what else to say." Lil E said

"Call yo peoples and see what she want to eat she wasn't answering for me." Nas said sounding a lil salty.

" she was with me no faking her ass got some shit up her sleeve, she was hella mad she had to come get me she said she was looking at properties." Lil E said seriously knowing his sister wasn't that type of girl.

They pulled into the lot as Lil E called his twin. " Aye Big Head ass girl what yo ass want from Lee's?"

" Damn yo ass rude as hell, you can get me spicey there piece mashed potatoes and red bean and rice ask for some strawberry jelly and honey, oh get a large sweet tea with extra ice." Niece replied playing no games as she worked up and appetite off the good news she had gotten.

" Damn, I'm too mad yo ass was that ready." Lil E said laughing.

" Where Nas at you still with him why he so quite?" Niece Questioned as to why he wasn't the one who was calling her for her order.

Before Lil E could answer Nas cut him off being and ass whole.

" I'm here I had to make sure I remember what you was getting, I was recording." He said sarcastically.

" why thanks my love , and I come down and get my food when yall get here if you want." Niece replied letting it be known she meant business.

" I'm a call you when you get downstairs then." Nas replied.

"Mannnn bye Niece we a see you when we get der." Lil E said and hung up. " Now you know yall need to stop, she really was in between a rock and a hard places today." Lil E said trying to get Nas to come around. " we gonna count this as the first fight with many more to come."

"Yeah you got that, I do be thinking way too much but lets get this food." Nas said as he pulled up to the speaker he made sure he order everything Niece wanted first then got Lil E and his stuff. Once they pulled off from the speaker he continued with the conversation. " Good thing I know she got brains and she aint one of these lames I think

I would of went crazy, I think its just the way the whole day went. It was the first time I spent that much time with Rah- Rah and it really hit me bra I broke down and it was just me and her." Nas said honestly.

" Yeah just know today was good day, don't feel bad about nothing that happened today you cant control how the life dice roll." Lil E said convincing Nas everything really did happen for a reason.

They sat in silence on the way back to the hospital they really didn't know what else to say to each other at this point, it was a good day as they say back and thought about the way shit played out. When they finally made it to the hospital they Lil thought it a be a good idea to go up and eat considering the fact his sister was on some bullshit and his broyo was too.

" you want me to take her ass this food or you coming up?" Lil E question to make it known he aint have time for they bullshit.

" Broyo you know im going up she crazy but I aint tryna see insane her ass was just to calm." Nas said laughing at how Niece handled the situation.

" I like the way you think my Brother." Lil E said laughing knowing great minds think alike.

When they made it back to the room Niece was on her laptop as usually and she didn't miss a beat as she looked up from the aroma of the chicken. " Yesss come through." She said put her hand in the air and sitting her lap top on the window seal.

" Why you gotta be so damn ghetto where ever yo ass go." Lil E said shaking his head trying to keep a straight face.

" im just saying yall right on time, thanks My Love." She and gave Nas a kiss as she took her food and drink.

" You welcome My Love." Nas said as he watched her back to her seat. " And she aint ghetto, she just a lil loud but I love it ." He said pulling up a seat next to Lil E.

" Nigga take yo ass over der by her too I don't care how tight the conner is." Lil E said messing with Nas.

" aw you know it aint a problem for me and you to switch spots." Niece replied with a lil laugh.

" yeah we most definitely can, I know you my sister at this point." Lil E said to his twin with a laugh.

Niece got her food and drink and started to switched seats with her twin. " aye you want to switch me stops or you done eating?" Niece asked with a laugh.

"we can most def switch seats." Lil E said grabbing his drink and the lil food he did have left being he was on a low key celebration, and she wasn't bout to mess that up. As he sat by Rah- Rah he damn near started to cry he looked at her and shook his head he still cant get it in his head that his lil sister straight in a hospital bed. " I don't see how they can just sit up in the hospital like this all day." Lil E said to his self as he finally took his seat.

When everyone was finally done eat Niece thought it would be a good time for a meeting. " So being we or trying to start and Organization, I think its time we really think a lil smarter." Niece said look from Nas to Lil E. " I mean you need to keep your hands clean, if you know what I mean. I cant risk losing no one else." Niece said looking at her best friend.

" You right and I respect that. We a be more careful and you got my word on that." Lil E said to his twin.

"So you sure you remember where the park at SK?" Nas asked, it had been almost two weeks and they still haven't seen or heard anything regarding the last lil incident.

"yeah I have a picture-perfect memory I just need to go some where one time and I wont forget." Sk said honestly.

"yeah it sound nice to have." Lil E said from the back seat. "And you know he just gotta make an extra stop."

" aye we need to make sure Big Bobby moms good first, then we on all Bs I aint play, we wouldn't have to bring our ass over here if they wouldn't have did Big B like that" Nas said making a very valid point.

" I don't know if you thinking with your heart or just for revenge." Sk said shaking his head at the point Nas just made.

" See I told you and then you got this muther fucking picture perfect memory." Lil E said shaking his head.

" I know we aint post to get into nothing but I think kind of personal." Nas said thinking about the fact it was a park and the only thing that a save them would be the fact of kids.

" well lets make sure we handle business first we gotta check on Ms. Roberson cool first. She is the main reason we over here." Sk said making sure they understood it was time she knew or had some type of closure regarding her only child.

" aye I told you we wouldn't be over here if it wasn't for they assed so with that being said we have nothing but good intentions and im giving her my number and every time I got come over here I am going to make sure they silly asses feel me on some level." Nas said seriously.

" Aye you know im with you when you right or wrong but especially when you right." Lil E said with his hands in the air.

"Yeah I don't think us three need to hang together. Its always going to be some bullshit only cuz we with the shits." Sk said laughing.

As they pulled up to the Ms. Roberson's they made sure that they guns was put up, being they didn't want to scare the old lady. Sk was the one to knock on the door.

" Hello Ms. Roberson, my nam is Sam I'm a friend of your son Bobby." Sk said as the old lady peeked from behind the door.

" Hey Sweety how you doing he told me I might be hearing from you, I didn't think it a take this long." Ms Roberson said inviting them all in.

" Thank you." They all said at once.

Ms Roberson turned and started shaking her head. " I know it was going to be something, he told me it was I talk to my child on a daily." Ms Roberson said. " I already filed the missing person report but I guess I should let it be a cold case?" She questioned the three already being hip to the out come.

"whatever it is you want us to do." Lil E said honestly, I can give you my number but you know like I know we not playing no police games.

" I can said the same." Nas mentioned to insure ms. Roberson she would be ok.

" it's been real strange since I got that helping hand , I told him and he showed me that most defiantly had something to do with me, we had our talk and that's when he told me if anything was to happen to him some kind men would insure me everything would be ok, you know how many visit I had before today?" Ms. Roberson stated. " I'm a good judge of character and that much he do know. I trust his last wishes, I don't know noting about nothing the same as you all do," MS Roberson mentioned being the police still haven't followed up with her regarding her only child.

After leaving Ms. Roberson's the ride was some what silent except for when Sk made the announcement that they were finally coming up on the park. " aye keep yall face up." Sk said letting Nas and Lil E know.

"Awwwww shit it most defiantly a no go!" Nas said as he watched a kid come down the slide.

" What a the fuck, hit a cut or something these niggas gonna feel something." Lil E said bouncing in the back seat.

" I was thinking the same thing." Sk said as he pulled in to the lot Big B got him hipped to.

" This some cut." Nas said as he peeped the whole park out of site, Big Bobby was on his toes." He said shaking his head.

" He knew something was up cuz this one hell of a cut." Lil E said putting everything together.

" On me it had to be." Sk chimed in replaying the day in his head.

They watched the kids play and decided that they should handle the situation another day.

* *

Mellow had a private service and they all decided to have the repast at the park being everybody had kids but him. JStacks knew he was relocating after all of the bullshit. Trey was going his own way after everything that happened. "yeah its most def I relocate." Jstacks said to his self as he watched a car pull off from over the hill. He watched as Trey played with the kids and started wondering if that was the reason he was still breathing. " yo Trey any day." Jstacks said giving him the signal he was ready to head out.

" I Just came to play" Lil Trey said laughing at how his response rhymed.

" I got a Sk" JStacks replied shaking his head.

" Aw ok just let it..."

" don't start." JStacks cut Trey off as he started to rap.

" it just seem like you amped it up." Trey said laughing.

"Yeah its time to go, you and me both gotta be tripping." JStacks said watching Trey move on his leg.

" ol girl on her way as we speak trust me." Trey said why shaking his head. "He gotta know I got me and mines why we out here." Trey thought to himself as he looked at

Stacks. Catching his self on his leg he grab his cruch with his good hand. "Aye lil big head lets head to the car yo momma shouldn't be that far." Trey said to his lil twin.

They made they way to Trey car in the lower parking lot of the park. They sat for about a good 5-10 mins before Trey girlfriend came in. He gave his son a kiss and hug put him in his car seat of his moms car and walked off.

" Yall so peaceful." JStacks said referring to Trey and his Bm.

" It took a while but she still cant stand me you see her ass don't even speak." Trey said shaking his head. " But you want me to drive or you driving." He asked Stacks getting to the point at hand It had been a good two weeks and he was back in motion after being put on bed rest. He wanted his lick back and he couldn't stomach the fact of Mellow being gone.

" I still don't see how yo ass drive with a leg like that." JStacks mentioned looking at Trey leg and one good hand.

"Aye bra this leg or this hand aint stopping shit. I can shoot and drive if you need me too." Trey said with a lil bounce.

" Yeah you on a whole lot of bullshit I see." Jstacks replied shaking his head.

" naw for real I can still use this hand and shit a lil bit." Trey said putting his left arm halfway in the air.

" You can drive then you want to drive yo shit or mines." JStacks asked Trey.

" Aw you the G8 you know I been wanting to push that mother fucker why you playing with with me right now?" Trey responded playfully.

" Say less, and yo ass bet not reck." Jstacks reached in his pocked and threw Trey the keys.

" You know I be backseat driving." Trey mentioned the scene" when everything had happened. He was watching everything why he was in the back seat, he even seen when dude let the window down and starting shoot the heat. Him and Mellow was on the same car the whole time.

" Yeah ill give you that yo ass put Mellow on game that day." Stack shook his head and got in the passenger side of the car.

The ride to the other side was quick for the simple fact the G8 and Trey became best friends he handle the wheel very well despite the condition he was in.

"Ok I see you really do got that wheel, you ever think about what if you was driving thst day? I mean seeing you handle the wheel now, I see why you asked the questions you asked. Why you just aint ask me to drive!" JStacks said excitedly looking over at Trey.

" Aye today is a new day, that's all I can say." Trey said shaking his head at the fact Mellow just might have still been around if he was driving.

" Man I know it was them niggas Big B usta call them some big tippers like they had the bag, who else gonna ge on our ass in a Jag." Jstacks asked putting everything together being they was in the same truck they killed Big B in.

" Its cool they gonna be looking like some fools when we catch they ass down bad." Trey stated with a lot of passion in his voice.

They made they way to the spot they was original at and still it was like a ghost town no one was in site.

" what the hell going on it like its work being down." Trey said as he made the left down.

As they got to the top of the street they had to turn around they didn't know which way to go so Trey decided to make a right he rolled by a couple of streets and made a left on one called Cabanne, he noticed a lot of houses but one stood out, it was the one with guys on the porch.

" they asses be outside I see." Jstacks said breaking Trey concentration and the silence.

They barely made off the street as Trey let the windows down and told JStacks to buck the heat but they was to late mother fuckers came out the cut and started fucking them up. Bullets came flying at the back of the car busting the back window out and some came through the trunk. Trey smashed on the gas trying to get away from they ass and almost crash once he notice he was losing filling in his right arm.

" Bra you hit!" Jstacks said to Trey pull over.

Just as Trey Pulled over and Jstacks got in in the passenger seat Mother Fuckers came running from down the street bucking they heats. JStacks didn't even notice Trey slumped in the passenger seat as he yelled " Get the heat!"

"im hit big bra" Trey said gasping for air "and I don't think im going to make it this time."

"Fuck!" Jstacks yelled and pulled off the street as niggas came rushing down the street with the heats. " You hang in der lil bro you hear me, hang in der you gonna make it don't say that shit you got a kid to live for come on and fight bra you got this. Yo shorty need you bra keep fighting." Jstacks pulled up to the same hospital they took Mellow and him to, just a lil ways from where they was. AS they arrived to the hospital Trey was still breathing but he was going in and out of conscious. Jstacks didn't know what else to do so he just sat and waited. After about a hour or so they came out and pronounce Trey dead. Jstacks put his hands on his head rubbed them down his face, he really didn't know what to say at this point. All he wanted was revenge. "what the hell im a tell his BM he left with me and aint coming back man I gotta get my life on track." He thought to himself. JStack sat and waited for Trey belongings and told the police the same thing it must have been the wrong place wrong time type thing cuz they wasn't in anything. His ride back to the East side was long but he made a promise to his self he a be back with some Missouri plates and he was shooting at anything in his way, "it had to the plates that gave us away." He said out loud to his self.

****

" Man can you believe them niggas really tried that shit?" Sk asked Nas.

"They asses slow." Nas said laughing.

" This new stick is sick, I could wait to see the bullets leave this mother fucker." Lil E said referring the clear magazine he had just gotten.

" I know yall ass better not had made this block hot." Tracey one of the Og's said.

" Man fuck all that you really thing they asses coming really coming back, if they do yo ass better do what you gotta do cuz as you can see they had you?" Norman the triple Og stated to his younger brother.

" yeah iight." Tracey responded.

" on me Og I got you they asses a be back but we can move locations down der on Maple." Lil E sated making it known he always thought about the zone.

" How that's gonna work?" The Norman asked.

" we tryna get like you Big Nor we some what own that shit." Nas stated making it like he was just talking shit.

" Yeah iight yall asses better be careful down der, they asses aint coming back threw here they asses aint that stupid but it look like they was coming from that way." Big Nor said.

" Yeah they silly asses keep bring they ass over here with them damn Illinois plates creeping making shit so obvious." Lil E mentioned.

" shit lets relocate just in case, for all they know we could have been having a party they don't know how we rock." Nas said to the Gang.

" Lets go Big Bra you know im a rock with you." Lil E said to Nas

" Lets rock out with our cocks out the." One of the Lil Homies said laughing about the comment he just made.

" Yeah you most def gotta shake the block after that shit." Tracey the Og said shaking his head and laughing at the comment.

" Lets head them ways who ever want to slide yall can slide, yall see anything come this way hit my line and im a do the same." Nas said knowing his brother was the only one he needed.

Once they made it down the way they set shop up and had the geeks come that way. It had been one hell of a day they had a shoot out and it still hadn't been a cop in site. For some reason that just didn't sit right with Lil E.

"Aye this shit aint sitting right with me." Said Lil E

" Aw man why you have to say that shit Lil E." Nas said shaking his head

" Im just saying bra, you know I had to let you know." Lil E said watching his brother head.

Just as Lil E said what he said he noticed a car pulling from down the street. The car stop and let the window down. They had the Lil Homie go to the car to serve the geek, that was the way he made his money.

" Aye watch that car lil homie and don't get to close." Said Lil E

" light im a just see what they need, im a come back and get the shit." Said Lil Mo he walked down to the car and ask form the sidewalk " what you need?"

" I need a 50$ ball." Jstacks said from the car he was in solo

Lil Mo ran back up the steps and said " he want a 50$ but it don't look like he do the shit I don't trust it."

Jstacks hopped out the driver seat with the chopper and let the bluts spray and got out the way.

Lucky Lil E seen his face he tried to get everybody out the way, but it was to late Nas got hit dead in his face, and Lil Mo was threw he got hit all in the back tryna get to his strap.

" what the fuck!" he yelled as he made his way to Nas and Lil Mo seeing them out der like that made him have flash backs. He notice the dude face was the one talking all loud when they came in the store that night. He had to talking about Big B, he new what he had to do. So many thoughts got to running through his head, like what he was going to tell his sister first Rah-Rah, now Nas, her ass bout to ready to get outside. He made a quick call to Sk so he could come get him out the way, he took the dope and guns before the police made it to the seen. Being they owned the property the police just assumed it was a mistaking identity.

"Man Lil Bra what the hell why yall asses aint been called me Norman told me yall went down the street but I aint think it was on some other shit!" Sk said angrily.

"Man Big Bra them Niggas came back aging and I let the ass have it, I knew something was up but everything just happened so fast I couldn't even get on his ass." Lil E said to Sk "the nigga was sliding by his self, you most def hit some shit both times." He said to Lil E

"That shit really makes me think." Lil E stated

"What you mean Lil Bro?" Sk questioned him.

" I straight feel my twin pain, it's like she Dr. Jekyll and im Mr. Hyde." Said Lil E .

" damn that's deep lil bra, I knew yall was close but I swear I aint know yall was twins." Sk said shaking his head.

" we just don't look alike cuz we wasn't in the same thing, you know how that shit go." Lil E said laughing at the fact most people really didn't know him and his where twins.

" Man yo ass told me that was yo lil sister." Sk said looking at the gine on Lil E face.

" Yeah I just came out before she did." Lil E said shaking his head at the fact Nas was the only one who really knew and he never said a word about shit. " Nas and Rah- Rah really the only people who knew."

After that comment the went straight to the hospital in silence being Lil E would have to be the one to tell Niece that Nas was dead. He knew she wasn't going to take it easy. He started thinking if he should even tell her being Nas and Rah-Rah didn't have any family, he could lay him to rest and not even say nothing else but he knew that wouldn't be the right thing to do considering the fact Rah- Rah could always come back too.

****

Jstacks ride back was somewhat peaceful he was out the way one Trey had his funeral, he was going to Miami fuck going to Atlanta he wanted to live on a beach. He made the all the necessary calls and everything was taking care of thank to Trey's BM. She really was hurt despite the relationship her and Trey had.

Trey home going was peaceful and they had the repast at the park they had Mellow's at. When everything was said and done JStacks took off leaving everything and everybody he had numbers on the people he needed, and he would be sure to send money for Trey being he did have a child.

When JStacks relocated he knew it was going to be easy, he had more than enough money saved, and it wasn't shit to get a lil spot and chill. He decided he wanted a fresh start so he knew he would have to look for jobs and even take some classes for real estate. He wanted to make keep his brother name alive and do something positive.

* *

Once Lil E hit the door with Sk it was nothing more really left to say. Niece had been call Nas phone damn near all day and he only responded with a text that said " I will love you always and forever, please don't me mad at me." She knew it was some shit but she felt her brother hurt and seen the pain in his eyes. She knew right then Nas was dead. She drop to the side of her best friends bed and just cried.

He brother came running to her side to comfort her and started crying his self, but he did let her see. He held her tight and rocked with her back and forth on the floor. He knew she knew. " I got you, I always got. It aint nothing we wont get threw you hear me." Lil E said picking Niece face up and looking her in eyes. He shook his head and stood up helping his twin to her feet. He knew she would never be the same after this one.

" We all gonna get threw this together and I can promise you that baby girl." Sk said taking everything in. He couldn't imagine the pain she was feel but looking her in her eyes he seen something had died inside her.

" thanks Big Bra." Said Lil E

" im leaving after this shit over E." Niece said looking and focused on her friend laying in the hospital bed.

" What you mean you leaving." Lil E asked.

" Well me and A-T, I got some business to handle and I needed you and Nas to stay here and handle the properties we have here." Niece asked with a blank look on her face.

" Now isn't the place or time for these yall got enough to worry about as it is." SK chimed in.

" you think I can see him at all?" Niece asked openly being her head a thousand and one places.

" Honestly sis I don't really think you want to, I seen it and I can forget it." Lil E stated

" Lets go get some air so we can talk about some shit." Niece said coming somewhat back to earth.

"yeah that do sound like a good idea." Sk agreed

" iight sis lets go." Lil E replied know she needed to let off some steam and was hoping she didn't want to plat 21 question about the situation.

Lil E watched his sister as they made they way outside and he felt more pain than he think he had ever felt. He seen the hurt and felt the pain, he knew she would never be the same after this. He seen something in her eyes he never seen before and it didn't give him a good vibe, she wanted revenge.

Sk decided to break the ice, " Aye I aint know yall had property Lil Bro."

" I don't she do well her and Rah-Rah that is." Lil E said shaking his head.

" That's the way to do it, I see yall hustling for a purpose." Sk said.

" yeah we most def aint tryna do this shit forever." Niece finally chimed in.

" I like yall lil team its solid." Sk responded. " and I can see who was the brains behind the whole thing."

" we all had the same amount of in put I guess you can say, we all believe in each other and thats what makes us so solid." Niece stated.

Once they made it outside Niece didn't want to play twenty-one questions, she want to teach somebody a lesson. She knew Karma would run its course but the way she was feeling she needed to let off some steam. " Im tired of the same ol shit Bra, my heart is hurting and I want somebody to feel my pain!" Niece stated boldly when they was walking up on a good spot to talk.

" Well now that its out der, when you tryna get outside you know you usual leave all violence up to me." Lil E questioned his twin.

" I'm ready when ever you need me to be." Niece replied quickly.

" aye Lil E I like the way she think, yall know im riding till the wheels fall off we all tied in now." Sk reminded them.

" Yeah I aint gotta question yo loyalty I know that much Big Bra." Lil E said reassuring SK he was still good on his end.

" That's really good to hear why im standing here, your going to need someone to help with everything that's going on." Niece said trying to focus on to much at once.

" Aw yeah that reminds me whats with these you leaving shit, where you going?" Lil E asked seriously.

" well I been doing some online auctions and I found some places out of state, Me and A-T was going to go but I don't even know if I want to go for business at this point." Niece said Honestly.

" I think that a be something good for yall two to do together, we still need to call and let her know whats going on with Nas too." Lil E stated

" Yeah and I don't think she going to take it well at all." Niece said shaking her head in disbelief.

" St.Louis one hating ass city baby girl, you need to leave any chance you get!" Sk said boldly. " You can make it a business trip but it has more meaning now, let this motivate you and make you go harder." He said with a lot of meaning.

" Yeah I guess I can hold it don't and lay low why you gone, you know I hate hospitals but I can suck it up. I'm a make sure Rah-Rah good why yall gone." Lil E finally said

" I got yall Lil Bra, you know Nas was like a brother to me as well." Sk stated.

The Three of them sat outside for few hours before they decided to go they separate ways. Niece decided to stay the hospital with her best friend and Lil E went home and cried to his A-T, being she took it much better than he expected surprisingly.

All Nas funeral arrangements where made from the hospital. Euniece wanted to make sure her friend was with her ever set of the way. As sad as it was she still wanted and needed her input on these kind of things. After all he was the only brother Rah-Rah had and she couldn't even be able to attend it. She knew what she had to do.

Niece made sure Nas went out like a true King. It was simple yet very elegant. The theme her and Lil E finally decided on was an all-white, for some reason he figured you couldn't go wrong with it. Niece did go all out of course she had to be extra extra, she made sure he had a white horse and clear carriage so you could see his white casket with the rose gold trimming and the 3 white doves was a must at the cemetery. Niece, Lil E, A-T and even Sk had a lot of in put on the funeral but the turnout was nothing like any of them had expected. Maybe it was because Niece always wanted to do the right thing Lil Moe and his family had no life insurance of course so she felt it was only right they had his before. Nas really brought the whole city out and Niece made sure everything was being recorded. It was most definitely a moment to remember. The most important thing that stood out was it was peaceful no fighting, arguing, or none of the extra shit when people like to fall out or cause a who is that kind of scene. A True King he was.

CHAPTER 7

Niece gave herself a couple of weeks before she decided to leave. She want to make sure Lil E and Sk was going to stay out the way and handle business being her and A-T was going to be gone it was like a free for all. Niece decided to have a sit down being it was a lot of property left that Lil E didn't know about. Niece had lots and all kinds of things set up to get renovated. Lil E felt she was hating considering the fact construction was his thing, she knew he could find a team or get one himself.

" So you mean to tell me you brought more properties than the one we all knew about?" Lil E finally asked

" Just a few lots and spots." Niece said innocently trying to not make Lil E upset.

" Whats a few Lots and Spots, Euniece?" Lil E asked looking his twin up and down

" Come on now with the government Lil E, a few lots on for a car lot and or tire shop and I have not figured out what I wanted to do with the other one. But I told you I just bied on stuff Lil E it don't even cost a lot of money, I guess because it shit in the hood and people think it aint no good, but I got hope and a lot of faith in us." Niece said boldly making a statement letting her brother know she meant business.

" She aint got time for your fuck up Lil E." Sk Finally stepped up and said with a lil laugh

" Aw is that what it is don't leave me then." Lil E said shrugging his shoulders.

" See here you go tripping and shit man bra pull it together im not going to stay and leave you with these people, no offense SK, you know you good in my book but make sure you check on ya peoples why we gone." Niece said patting Lil E on the shoulder shaking her head laughing.

" I'm glade yo big head ass think its funny, im a come find ya asses yall take too long." Lil E said finally coming around.

" And im a make sure I hold it down why he go or we might just shut some shit down and come raise hell together."Sk said making a statement.

" See that's the shit im talking about right der she got us fucked up." Lil E said with a lil smile.

" Its good to see you smile bra." Niece said. "Now that we got that out the way, I'll be sure to check in." Niece said using her fingers making quotation marks.

" Thank you that's all I ask Euniece." Lil E said mocking her.

Niece and A-T took a late flight that way they could sleep on the plane ride, Niece made sure to let him track her location that way she aint have to check in as often she knew he would turn his off being they always thought it was federal. " that thought made her laugh being she never did know where him and Nas ass would be at." She was starting to look at things in a whole different way.

" You doing ok baby girl?" A-t asked like she was in her head braking her thoughts.

" Yeah the way I be think about things be scaring me ." Niece said turning her head looking A-T in her face.

" Tell me a little bit more about what you mean." A-t said very interested. Her and Niece never really got to talk about anything, it was like she was avoiding her for some reason.

" A-t I just honestly feel like all this is my fault. I mean I know people tell me not to blame my self but I can' t. I mean if I wasn't so quick to pop off and punch dude Rah-Rah wouldn't even be in the hospital. It's a lot of blood on my hands and I know he just out here living life." Niece turned and looked out the window of the plan at the night sky it was so clear.

" You going to feel how you feel regardless and cant nobody change that but you. That's if you want to that is. Its a lot to think about and trying to understand that way God works will drive you crazy baby girl. He the only one who knows your path in life and everything happens for a reasons, its best you just go with the flow." A-T said holding Niece hand tightly.

" I Love you A-T, you always know just what to say." Niece said returning the tight hold letting her know she would be ok.

The rest of the way they slept, then came the over lay for the last fight it wasn't that long, but she couldn't sleep the rest of the way. She just listened to music and did some more planning; it was too much on her mind to really sleep. When they finally made it to their destination it was almost day light aging. See the sun set and rise was a site to remember it was such a beautiful thing. She knew she was ready for what ever it was God had in store for her and all her loved ones. It was peaceful as ever.

They decided to go with an Air BN, it was really nice a lil two bed room house in a low key area. Just as Niece was about to check in she got a facetime from Lil E.

" So that's why you aint tell me where yall asses was going you knew I wanted to put my feet in some mother fucking sand."

" Can we get settled in!" A-T said from the background

" Naw I aint messing with you either cuz you know too." Lil E said with a big grin.

" Seeee that's why I mess with you A-T it all business bra nothing personal, you already aint got ya mind right and you aint even here with me. We aint even land and you talking about some sand, help me stay focused please." Niece relayed to Lil E cutting A-T off with the shocked face.

" Yeah iight send me some pictures Niece and I aint playing." Lil E said shaking his head. He was happy his sister was seeing better things. She was living her best life and it was good to see her finally really smile with out forcing it.

" You know I got you." Niece said

" Its good to see you smile baby girl." Lil E said to his twin.

" I love you Bra be safe please." Niece said to Lil E

" Love you more and no need to say please I know you got me." Lil E said and ended the facetime.

" Man A-T yo peoples crazy." Niece said, taking heed to what was just said.

" You knew him before he knew me, soooo..." A-T gave Niece some time to let what she just said sink in. They both laughed and went out and looked and the beautiful view they had. A-T took a quick picture and looked over at Niece and said " Now this one for you."

Niece already knew what that mean, off guards was the best so she just did a lil quick pose.

"Yeah all them was cute." A-T said shaking her head

"Yeah I need to know who got you so hip ." Niece said looking at A-T walking away slowly like she was watching her closely.

Once they got settled in Niece finally got some sleep, A-T made sure her meetings where set up for the next day. A-T knew something would change with plane ride. Everyone was very understanding being they where always on top of their game. It was peaceful night surprisingly. Niece actually got to sleep the night away

"I can't believe I actually got to sleep like that, why would you let me sleep like that is the question." Niece said feeling refreshed.

"You the one who needed the sleep. I made sure all your meetings where rescheduled for today same time as yesterday so I think you should get a Kobe on." A-T said honestly.

"Yeah you right, I didn't mind the sleep at all, thanks for taking care of everything for me." Niece said not knowing what she would do with out her.

"yeah the rental car a be here shortly so make sure you ready to go you know I ain't driving around here." A-t mentioned.

"So you just going to force me to drive like I actually know where I'm going we both from the same city ya do know that right." Niece said joking trying to hurry and find some business casual clothes.

It took A-T and Niece about 30 mins to get dress luckily the rental car drive was running late his self so everything worked out for both parties. They headed out side grabbed the keys and everybody went they own ways. They only had two appointments today only good thing about everything was it was with the same company.

"So today we just deciding which spot would be better to start with, they giving good prices considering the areas we got. I guess we have to see which one we like more." Niece told A-T to make sure she understood.

" I was wondering why you had different appointments with the same people, that's why they was so friendly." A-T said insuring Niece she understood

" Yeah I really do be trying to stay on top of things considering everything that's been going on. I try to keep them in the loop." Niece replied honestly.

" Welcome Ladies and thank you for coming!" The agent said to Niece and A-T.

" Thank you for having us." A-T said cutting Niece off shaking the fine young man hand.

" My apologies for the reschedule." Niece said shaking the mans hand and her head at the same time surprise at the these new woman her A-T had become.

" My name is Julius and I will be your real estate agent, if you all need anything don't hesitate to call me and let me know what's going on or if you have any question." Julius stated giving bot A-T and Niece his business cards why taking the lead to his desk.

" Now that's some kind of eye candy for you." A-T said to Niece tring to whisper.

" I think he can hear you, and I don't even like light skin men." Niece replied rolling her eyes in a playful way. This lady really is something, she thought to herself.

" Well maybe you should." A-T replied with a playful push.

Once they made it to Julius desk they went over the two properties they would be looking at. He made sure he they knew the price difference in both location and the areas where both really good being they where so close to the beach.

He spoke with his manager before the meeting and the decided if they got one property they a give them the other at a discounted price being the came all these way Julius knew they was about business.

" Being you ladies came all these way I was able to cut you all a deal if you couldn't decide on which location you liked more, it might be a tough to choose just one." Julius mentioned.

" Sounds good I guess great minds think a like however, I think it a be better to buy one and lease the other being we wont really be down here to manage things." Niece said letting Julius know he couldn't get in her head.

" Well with that being said did you need for me to follow you, or did you just want the code the keys a be in the lock box." Julius asked with surprise.

" The Code to the lock boxes a be fine, if we could see both that would be fine, I'll be sure to call with the notes and questions I have." Niece wouldn't know the statement she made until later off in life.

" Ok, well here's the codes the address is beside each one of them to make it easier for you, call me and let me know which one you decide on." Julius replied handing the codes and paper work over to Niece and A-T.

Once in the car Niece entered the addresses and the went to the closet one first. Julius was right both places was nice but Niece took it as saving the best for last, it was a bit more pricey but it was most defiantly worth it considering the location and the new set up.

" yeah I think we should with this one." A-T said like she was inside of Niece head.

" I was just thinking the same thing."Niece said with tears in her eyes.

" You want to make the call or should I?" A-T questioned

" You can call him you the one who want his number out side of business reasons." Niece replied messing with A-T.

Why A-T was making calls Niece deiced to check in with Lil E and just send him pictures of the properties and the little things they seen along the way. He was excited for her out of town making a brand and name, making sure Nas didn't go in vain. He had to Facetime her. " Now I think yall should go celebrate everything on me check ya cash app." Lil E told niece

" Aw shit you aint gotta tell me twice tell Sk send me a lil more and we can rent a place down here if that's the case." Niece said playfully with a big smile.

" Aye Niece stop playing with me get yo ass coming home even if I gotta come get you my damn self." Lil E said playing yet very serious.

" I got ya fam chill we will give a day or two and we should be back I gotta sign some paper work and shit im serious about the extra money doe, they tryna give us a deal on so stuff so just let me know what you think. Love you and be safe please."

" Love ya more baby girl and I most def will let you know what Sk talking bout." Lil said and hung up the phone.

" I really do love yall relationship." A-t said coming around the corner as Niece ended the call.

" You did raise up these way, it aint that many of us you know." Niece said, " How the call go?"

" well he was very excited to her from me and he said that he would be bring you the keys and papers to sign." A-t said playfully blushing and touching her chest and then rolling her eyes and throwing her hands up. " I guess he really do know im the assistant, he want you not me." She said laughing and shaking her head.

" Im not about to play with you right now lady, and why yo mind in the gutter at a time like these, these is post to be business nothing personal." Niece said and laughing with tears in her eyes.

" Aint nothing wrong with a lil personal business now is it?, you better live your life baby girl you only get one." A-t said seriously knowing Niece was still hurt she didn't want it to stop her from find happiness and love again.

Niece really didn't know what else to say so she just shook her head and walked off trying to play it off as if she was still laughing. She got out side and took everything in, the view, the smell, and the energy. It was a great feeling yet she still felt so empty, she was still angry she didn't have anyone to really celebrate with. She sat outside until the reality team came, they all took pictures of them giving Niece and A-t the keys and in front of the sold sign.

Julius decided to shoot his shot and invite Niece out to dinner to celebrate. He was still some what New in town but he still have really had a night out himself. He had been working his ass off trying to forget his past and everyone in it he so called himself doing a good deed and buying Euniece the addition property but he didn't want to tell her just yet. A new life is something he wanted and knew she was wife material, he seen she wanted a fresh start maybe she just need a little more support. He barely the night that changed his life but he made sure he took that as a lesson learned. He waited for his team to finally leave and he told them he wanted to make sure that both deals where secured so he could stay back.

" Miss Euniece would you like to go out and celebrate your closing today with me." Julius asked

Niece looked at A-t who gave her a you better look and she said " Yes, I would love too but I don't want to leave my Aunt in the hotel alone we need to be celebrating together."

" Oh no honey im beat, you two go enjoy the night we have many more times to come." A-t said to Niece making her way to car waving her off tell her to leave her out of it.

" well now that, that's out the way, I guess I would too. I can send you the address to the house we staying in." Niece said to Julius.

" Sounds great guess I can pick you up around 7, ifs that's ok with you." Julius finally got the words out. He made sure to treat her like the true Queen he knew she was, being she said yes that's all that mattered. She gave him hope for a better future.

" I Honestly cant not believe you a really leave me hanging like that A-T I have to admit, I thought we was so much better than that." Niece said looking at her surprised and shaking her head.

" Aw baby leave it up to me you always going to live yo best life I aint that old I know how to find my way around and have a good time honey stop worrying about everybody and live your life just a little." A-T said trying to talk all negative thoughts out of Niece's head.

" Yeah I guess you right but its hard ya know with everything going on I kind of feel guilty. I mean don't get me wrong the energy im feeling is crazy is just don't really know how to take it, its like im ready for whatever as strange as it may sound just going with the flow seems to work." Niece stated insuring A-t should try to have fun tonight.

" Good just go with the flow, but stay focused baby girl. Don't you ever feel bad about anything God has in store for you, he the only one who knows your path! I want you to try to enjoy your self to night. This is about you, at the end of the day we came all this way because of who?, You." A t replied with nothing but love hearing the response she just hear.

The rest of the way to the house was silent as usual when Niece felt to deep of a conversation coming on. She zoned out as usually and just took everything in think about everything from every which way. She really didn't understand the way things were playing out and the only thing she really could do was hope and pray. Going with the flow at this point seem like the right thing to do. She thought about everything she had packed in her suite case somewhat decided on two out fits she wanted to give A-T some piece of mind being it was going on 6.

When they finally got to the House Niece went straight for he suitcase and got to laying things out she really didn't need any help she decided on a pair of ripped up tight fitted capri jeans, and tight fitted tank top, and some platform sandals. The jeans fit her like a glove, she made sure she was comfortable being she didn't really know what these dude had planned.

" Ok now baby girl that's what I like to see you look like a real boss." A-T said walking in on Niece, she loved how she never really did to much but just enough. She noticed her anklet, and necklace with the earrings.

" Thanks A-T, I love your energy." Niece said laughing turning around in a circle with a lil pose.

" I texted Lil E earlier when I got in the car and he said he was on his way to the hospital to check on Rah-Rah he hasn't said anything then. And im going to send him the pictures when I know your good and gone so its no need to answer your phone." A-t made sure Niece knew she meant business.

" Yes ma'am I got you. And thank you so much I don't know what ill do without you!" Now that Niece knew that little did A-t know her phone was going on airplane mode. She was ready to enjoy herself and she was happy Julius was 15 mins early because she was already ready.

Julius was shocked at how simple yet classy Niece looked she was really ready for what Miami had in store for her. Lucky they was going to get a bit to eat and visit the beach.

" So you do know im still pretty new in town my self right?" Julisus said as Niece got in the car.

" Ok what that post to mean, you want me to get out your car or something." Niece said defensively not knowing how to take his statement.

" I was just saying I didn't really have anything important to do, well being with you is important but I didn't have time to really plan anything." Julius said stubbing all over his words.

Niece couldn't do anything but blush. " its ok it's the little things that matter to me." She said trying to apologize for the way she just came off.

" Well hopefully I cant make this a night to remember for you." Julius replied to nervous to say anything else. He Decided to changed some plans. " Did you eat anything at all?" Julius asked.

" Yeah we grabbed something before we went in." Niece said quickly being she didn't want anything to eat.

" Well we can go to the beach I still haven't been in the little time I have been down here." Julius honestly replied.

" Sounds good to me I don't really like clubs, people killed that whole vibe for me." Niece stated.

" Yeah I can say the same thing, I aint been out in I don't know how long. I told myself I was cool on a club until I could buy myself one. Julius said realizing she was the only one her ever really told that too.

" Sounds like a plan to me, ill help you manage it, that just might bring me back more often." Niece replied thinking about how they could really be a good business team.

" Yeah I think im a have to make that happen pretty fast then." Julius said thinking about the comment she had just made. He knew they a be a true power couple.

Chapter 8

When Julius and Niece finally woke up it was the next the morning. Julius was more than excited; this was the first time he spent the whole night with a girl and he didn't even try to make a move on her. He was happy with his self he knew he wanted to be different with Miss Euniece. He was happy he did do his good deed he felt as if it really paid off. He was able to slide the paperwork in with everything when he did go back to the office. Being it was Friday he didn't have to go back into the off until Monday, his boss told him to make sure that he celebrated considering the deals he just closed. He really was planning on spending his whole weekend with Niece and even the rest of his life if she wanted too.

Niece felt refreshed when she woke up, she took her phone off airplane mode and sure as shit all the calls and text messages started coming in. She knew it was A-t and Lil E so it was really no need to check every text. She shook her head and put the phone on the bed beside her.

" you must be really important." Julius said a lil jealously.

" No its just my Aunt and my Big Brother." Niece said with quotes.

" ohhh, my apologies guess you really don't get out much, you ready for me to drop you back off at your room." Julius asked.

" Yeah they gonna start back call I can feel it." Niece said looking at the phone she felt as if something was wrong.

They barely made it to the car before Lil E received a Facetime from Lil E. " where the fuck yo ass been Euniece, why you want to play with me, you know im literally on my way to the damn airport!" Lil E said angrily.

" Wow Lil E chill I'm with a friend, you told me to go celebrate." Niece replied sounding confused, she knew something wasn't right she felt the whole vibe change. " Im a call you when I get out this Man car, and stay yo ass where you at, I can handle myself." Niece replied hanging up the Facetime.

" Yeah you the baby girl I see, sorry if I got you into any kind of trouble." Julius responded.

Niece didn't know what it was about these guy but he was just to good to be true, maybe it was because he had a friendly face she felt comfortable with him but something wasn't starting to still right with Lil E flipping the way he did. " Naw I aint in trouble, my security get mad if they cant find me I post to had my location on." Niece said trying to come up with a lie to change the subject as always.

" I can most definitely understand I only had a little brother, can't imagine life with a sister God only knows the kind of woman she would have been." Julius said shaking his head with a evil grin.

" Really y'all was that bad grown up, you don't even look like that type?" Niece said with her eyebrows raised in the air looking at him sideways.

"Yeah we was something else, things happen and it make you change for the better I guess." Julius said winking at Niece. They enjoyed the rest of the ride to hotel talking about life goals and how they both wanted so much more in life. Julius knew Niece was the one for him, they even agreed on a dinner date later, him picking her up was still undecided being Niece Aunt was standing on the porch and she didn't look pleased.

"Yeah I'm a most definitely have to text you, she don't look happy." Niece said feeling like a kid who was about to get a whooping.

" Be safe Miss Eunice." Julius said laughing shaking his head and unlocking the doors for her to get out.

" Thanks for everything." She said and winked at Julius.

The walked to the porch made Niece smile fade she seen not only was A-T upset but she had been crying she was worried and Niece didn't even get one good foot in the house before she followed her in slamming the doors. Niece never seen A-T upset but it's a first time for everything.

"Niece you really had me worried sick and your brother don't make shit no better with his crazy talking ass got me thinking people kidding you and shit, you really need to call him he really worried about you and it's something he not tell me. I sent him pictures and it's like all hell broke loss he told me to find you and tell you get back here did you read any of your messages? The boy is crazy." A-T said rubbing the sides of her head from the migraine she had gotten.

"What happened is Rah-Rah ok, what you mean crazy talk what he tell you!" Niece asked frantically.

"Yes honest Rah-Rah is fine he said something about shaking hands with the an opp whatever that post to mean he was freaking out, steady tell me to have you call him, I told him I told you not to answer your phone and that just made things even worst honey." A-t kept going but Niece had zoned all the way out. "Niece or you listening to me it look like just seen a ghost."

"Yeah I need to go call Lil E and take an I'm a need a Nap after that." Niece honestly replied.

She read the text message A-t and Lil E had sent, he didn't really say to much but you could tell he was pressed about her not answering her phone. She took out her head phones and FaceTimed her twin. " Ok so what's really going on I know you can't say to much over the phone." Niece said when Lil E answered the phone.

"Finally yo ass decided to call me, I thought dude was on some sick shit and put yo ass on his hit list." Lil E said in the camera using a gun hand motion so Niece knew he was serious.

"What you mean Julius he's a nice guy it seems like he the one who was trying to give me the deal I was telling you about and what's the opp shit A-T talking about?" She questioned.

" I bet he was nice, I'm a let you think on it but you really do need to watch who you talk too. I'll fly back out when y'all get back so I can see what all work need to be done on my end."Lil E said in disbelief

" What you mean, now you got me thinking!" Niece said as her mind began to ramble.

"Just know you fucking with the opp and you need to be careful baby girl, handle ya business and get back so I can come handle mines." Lil E said and ended the FaceTime.

Damn! Niece thought to herself, I knew it had something to do with dude she thought long and hard on everything her twin had said. She knew Julius was now on the opp lost but why? She knew she need more information so she finally sent a text asking for the location to the place he wanted to meet. Luckily it was a place right down the way and it wasn't really too much of a drive. Trying to take a nap was out of the question he was ready to play 21 questions. She got ready easy, she was on a mission and didn't have any time to lose.

The location was a low place it was sushi bar being it was something they both wanted to try, they informed the server an idea of the things they wanted to try and Niece let Julius decide on the order. Once the food was out the way Niece tried to get some more information.

" So what was it you said you usta to do back in your hometown?" she asked

" I was a bad boy I guess you can say I usta sale drugs honestly just to make a way. Its nothing I'm proud of so I don't really talk about it." Julius replied honestly.

" Where you from if you don't mind me asking, you know i'm from St. Louis, what you got some secrets you need to keep." Niece asked playfully.

" I'm from Illinois or the Ill said as yall call it." Julius replied laughing at Niece " I don't have anything I want to keep from you Euniece I can promise you that. You can say I am an open book when it comes to you." Julius said looking deeplying into Niece's eyes.

Just as he did that the server was making her way back dropped a tray with food on it the noise caused Niece to just being it sounded like a gun shoot. She had a flash back and she couldn't believe what she was seeing, it couldn't be.

" Niece you ok." Julius asked reaching for Niece's hand

She jerked backed unexpectedly, " Yes im fine sorry that just really scared me." She didn't be believe in coincidences, it all made since to her the reason she came and not Lil E, the energy and, and even his friendly ass face. She couldn't believe herself and she knew why Lil E was so upset.

" What you shell shocked or something Lil Lady." Julius asked trying to lighting the move, but little did he know it only made things worst.

"Actually I am." Niece snapped. " was you ready to go I kind of lost my appetite."

" Sure we can, I didn't mean to disrespect you or make fun of you in any kind of way. I know that's some serious shit it kind of scared me myself. Just did want to seem soft ya know." Julius replied trying to cover it up. He felt things going down heal and he didn't want to end the night on a bad note. " Niece I really do like you and ill come to the Lou with you if you want me to do. I can take a few vacation days, if you want me to meet your brother I want him to understand that your in good hands and I wont let anything bad happen to you." Julius kept going.

Hearing what she just heard Niece mind started going every which way. It was crazy but she knew everything he had told her was true, she was the incident in the club that changed him and she knew he didn't remember. Niece made her mind up he was going to pay for everything he put her threw. Lil E a off his ass the first chance he got not giving a fuck who was around so bring him back was to risky not to mention his job a know who he's with.

" How about we just go back to the beach, I'm a just follow you I need to get my head together and it was so peaceful." Niece finally and honestly said.

"Sounds good to me, it was most likely our food she dropped so let just make a run for it." Julius replied standing and asking for Niece hand.

She placed her hand in his and stood up tall with her head high, you would of never knew what she was up to. " I'll follow you I should be able to drive." She said following Julius out the door to the cars.

Julius knew it would be now or never for him to tell Niece about the new place he secretly brought for her. He took the keys but left he paperwork in the office he did need a reason for her to come back everything was finalized and ready to go. Once they made it to niece quit corner of the beach Julius was able to get the words right out " I have a surprise for you."

" I don't really like surprise Julius, you seen that back at that place." Niece said shaking her head.

" it's a good one I promise." Julius said with his heads in the air.

" Yeah ok I guess we can go." Niece said going with the flow. Niece rode with him being she didn't want to throw things off. The ride to the surprise was pretty quiet being Niece was thinking about everything.

" you sure you ok, you don't seem like yourself today." Julius said trying to get in Euniece head.

" yeah just a lot on my mind we go home in the morning." Niece responded honestly.

" I think these surprise a make you want to visit a whole lot more." Julius said with a big grin.

"What you grinning so hard for?" Niece asked seriously.

" you a see." Julius replied.

When they finally pulled up to the place Niece didn't really know what to say she noticed they dropped one of those huge dumpster off and a sold sign on the grass. She got out the car and noticed Julius had a set of keys. " your kidding me." Niece said unexpectedly with a look of disbelief on her face.

" No I'm not and it's not for the club thing, I seen the drive you have and I couldn't let's you miss out a blessing, I know you a know what to do with this place." Julius said handling Euniece the keys.

" I can't take these." Niece said trying to give the keys back.

"What you mean girl you better keep them keys."!Julius said. He made his way to the door and waited for Euniece to let them in.

She did as she was told and did the walk threw taking notes of things. When Julius finally opened the basement door he went flying down the steps and landed with a hard bang, he was out. She found so rope and tape and made some shit shake with what she could. She knew what she had to do so she waited for him to come too.

"What did I ever do to you?" Julius asked when he finally came too.

" you really don't remember do you?" Niece questioned.

" I ain't never seen you!" Julius yelled.

Niece put tape of his mouth. " well you see you remember that night in the club you was telling me about that changed your life. That was me. The girls you shot at that night that was me. You see I didn't notice cuz I'm guess you cut your hair and changed your look. I been praying you feel the pain that I feel and here you is right in my face. I knew it was something with you, I knew you was to good to be true. You took my soulmate the only man I will ever love. You really thought you was going to play me after all you did to my family?" Niece didn't really have to much more to say, seeing the look on his face let know he understood everything.

Julius didn't have anything to say when she finally did remove the tape. He looked her in the face and told her " I apologize for everything I put you threw." Jstacks knew he could no longer run from the things he did that one night. He knew it was something about Euniece he just didn't expect her to be so cold hearted. She didn't even give him a chance to tell her the house and paperwork was all in her name.

She wiped the keys off and put them back in his pocket. " I don't want anything from you." Niece said in his ear. She stepped back shock her head damn I thought it was love at first sight, guess I aint take none of them signs right. Should have know you only get one real love in a lifetime." She made he way up the stairs and Julius could nothing but watch. On her way out the door she notice the gas stove and turned it on until she heard the ticks and make her way out. Hopefully no one found him before the house blew up, she want him to go from the carbon monoxide first.

She made her way back down to the beach so she could get her car and pack up to head home. She felt as if she handled all business necessary at this point. It was a long night for Niece and a even longer flight. Knowing she took a life just didn't feel right. Her mind was all over the place being she really did have good intentions behind everything, she knew she was still grieving and she aint have no business messing with that man. Trying to rush thing and look at what happen she thought to herself. She knew what she had to do and followed threw with, she started it all so it was only right she was the one to end it.

When they finally landed Lil E and Sk was waiting at the gates for Niece and A-T. "What the hell they whispering about?" A-t asked Niece being she was quite the whole way and she was shocked to see SK.

"Who knows they asses always up to something." Niece finally said to A-t.

Before Lil E could get a word out he literally ran to Niece and gave her the biggest huge ever, he felt her energy and he knew it wasn't good, she seem hurt even. " Damn Baby girl what the hell you do why you was down der?" Lil E said look Niece up and down.

" I did what I had to do." Niece said and headed for the exit.

" what you mean you" Lil E asked chasing behind her leave S-k with A-t .

" I did what I was post to do thanks to you. I never wouldn't have knew anything. I think I killed him." Niece finally came out and said

" What you mean think? And you post to leave that kind of shit up to me, that was personal Niece I was going to handle that." Lil E said shaking his actually hoping he was dead so he could be the one to kill him.

Just as they stepped out of the airport Niece got a phone call. " oh heavens no, I haven't seen or heard from him since we signed on the properties. He told me he was going to celebrate, what happened if you don't mind me asking is everything ok?" Niece asked the real-estate team.

"Well the discounted property he sold you paperwork is still on his desk but the keys are gone, we where hoping he did a final walk threw with you being it looked as if everything was finalized. The fire department found his car outside but due to the gas leak everything went up in flames and they could save or find anything stating that he was even at the residence. Due to the unexpected situation we can find you another place or we can send you a full refund being we had insurance on the place still we can still work something out in your favor." Stated Julius boss.

" im guessing you can just send the money back to me and I will look for something else in the meantime, I jut got back home and I don't have time to fly back out again." Niece said as she got in front seat of the car.

"What was that about?" Everybody asked at once.

"nothing damn yall nosey." Niece replied.

The ride home was quite as usual being Niece wasn't the one to start the conversation.

Just before the made it to the house Niece phone rang again. This time it was the hospital. They told Niece it was nothing more they could do for Rah- Rah at this point and they had to take her off the machines. " what do you mean you taking her off the machines and you know that's the only thing helping her?" Niece wish she could have push the words back in because not the whole car was looking at her. She did cry she simple told he twin. " Take me to the hospital." I need to face my raw reality."

Lil E didn't say a thing he just did as he was told, once they all made it the Doctors told them she had be came brain dead meaning her brain had complete stop responding. It was nothing more left to say. Rah- Rah and Nas was the only two kids and they moms had died back in the day that's what made them so close. Niece knew her friend was tired of fighting it was far she had to suffer the way she was. She was with the two people she loved the most. Niece knew she wouldn't be the same after everything and she felt kind of bad for Julius being it seem like he really was will to change, but Karma don't have no time limit.

" you cool baby girl ." Lil E said breaking her thoughts. He see the expression on her face and knew she would never be the same.

" Naw bra I aint but I will be, I got my Personal Guarding Angles watching over me." Niece replied.

Lil E and Niece decided that they want to stay so Sk took A-t home she said that was something she didn't want to see and he couldn't do nothing but respect her for that.

" I knew it was going to come to this." Niece said breaking the silence.

" Deliberate a little bit more for me, because I aint really had no wired feelings since Nas and I most definitely aint see this one coming Sis." Lil E said with tears in his eyes.

" Don't cry bra she in a better place he in a better place, you know they all a family again. I'm glad I was the one to get dude doe, I felt like I talked all that shit and got to get my lick back I know it sound crazy but it was Karma for his ass." Niece said trying not to cry.

" Yeah Karma right in the Flesh for his ass." Lil E said shaking his head in disbelief.